T0047151

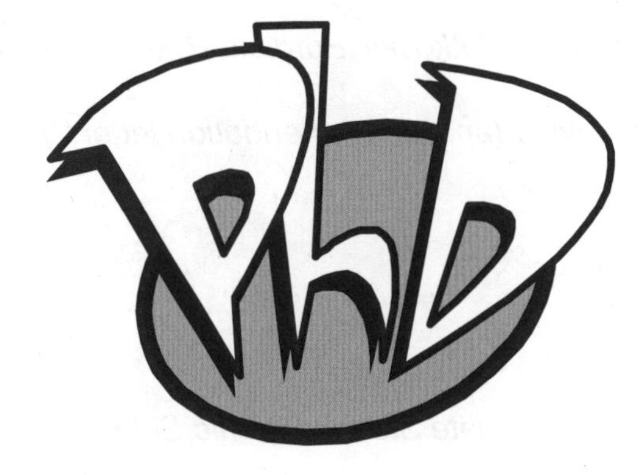
PhD

This book is dedicated to Professors Cutkosky, Burdick, Roth, Book, Mistree and Herod:

Thanks for your teaching and advice (and recommendation letters!).

Other books by Jorge Cham:

"Piled Higher and Deeper: A Graduate Student Comic Strip Collection"

"Life is Tough and then You Graduate: The Second Piled Higher and Deeper Comic Strip Collection"

"Scooped! The Third Piled Higher and Deeper Comic Strip Collection"

"Adventures in Thesisland: The Fifth Piled Higher and Deeper Comic Strip Collection"

"We Have No Idea: A Guide To The Unknown Universe"

Academic Stimulus Package

The Fourth *Piled Higher & Deeper* Comic Strip Collection

by

Jorge Cham

Piled Higher and Deeper Publishing
Los Angeles, California

Academic Stimulus Package: The Fourth Piled Higher and Deeper Comic Strip Collection

Published by Piled Higher & Deeper, LLC
Los Angeles, California

www.phdcomics.com

Third Printing, October 2017
PRINTED IN CANADA

ISBN-10: 0-9721695-4-7
ISBN-13: 978-0-9721695-4-7

Library of Congress Control Number: 2009901097

The Uncertainty of Hope
An Introduction not by Barack Obama

They said this day would never come. We were told that we could not do this. That our sights were set too low, that we faced impossible odds, that we would never find enough material for a fourth PHD book.

Yes we did.

You see, this is not about me. I mean, it's mostly about me. But it's also about you. In the unlikely (or is it unlikeable?) story that is Academia, there has never been anything false about the proverbial "we."

It is what pushed bands of academics to create over 20,000 different journals worldwide and it is what pushed Jorge Cham to continue writing this comic. In the darkest of nights, against insurmountable writer's block, when it seemed that no further humor could be found in the graduate student experience, something started to happen. Generations of grad students responded with the cautious creed that sums up the spirit of an institution: Yes, we might.

Yes we might get significant results. Yes we might graduate (someday). Yes we might send Jorge stories about my advisor and my co-workers so that he might make fun of them on his website. Yes we might invite him to come speak at our University.

Many of the stories they shared are the stories in this book. In the darkest of nights (did I say that already?), in the long hours at the lab, their sighs joined together as one sigh. And in the uncertainty in their voice we learned that the struggles of the molecular biologist at U. Washington are not so different than the plight of the Proust scholar at Princeton. We learned that the hopes of the master's student who goes to the crumbling History department in U. Kansas are the same as the dreams of the PostDoc who learns on the streets of UCLA.

It turns out, grad students are one people. Hopeful, dorky, unsure of why they signed up for this, but optimistic nonetheless. Optimistic about optimal results, positive about positive trials and confident about significant confidence intervals. What began as a simple comic in the Stanford Daily newspaper has swelled, click by click, into a chorus of literally millions (see the last page of this book).

The road ahead remains less clear. The smallness of our problems may outlast the size of our departmental politics. But always remember this: Nothing can stand in the way of millions of grad students, procrastinating. So if you are ready for more of the same, but different. If you will send in your comic suggestions when you should be working instead. If you will forward the comic to everyone you know, we will begin the next great chapter in the PHD saga, with three words that will ring from campus to campus, from quad to shining bell tower: Yes we might.

Yes we might.

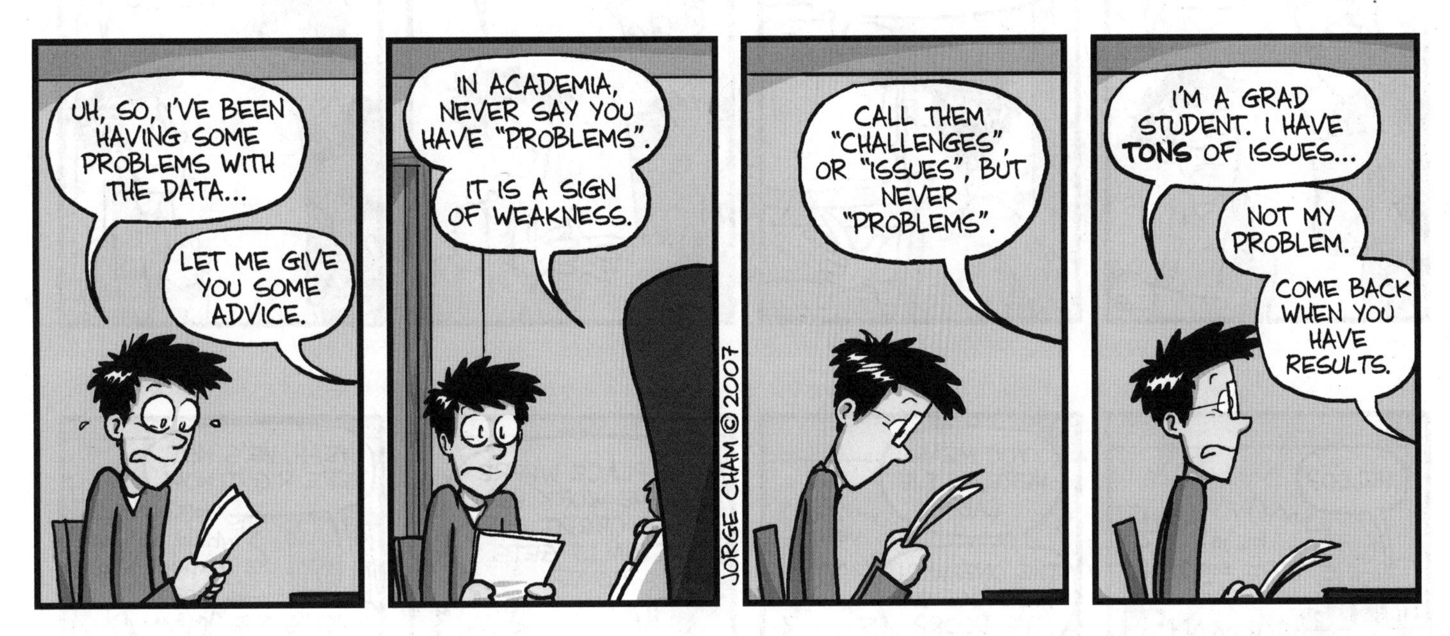

COMIC STRIPS
2007-2009

DID YOU GET MY E-MAIL?
UH, WHICH ACCOUNT DID YOU SEND IT TO?
I HAVE A WORK E-MAIL, A PERSONAL E-MAIL, AN ONLINE SHOPPING E-MAIL, MY UNDERGRAD E-MAIL, THE DEPARTMENT-ISSUED E-MAIL, MY INSTANT MESSAGE E-MAIL...
JORGE CHAM © 2007
I LIKE TO KEEP THINGS SEPARATED. IT MAINTAINS THE ILLUSION I'M IN CONTROL OF MY LIVES.
"LIVES"?
MULTIPLE PERSONALITIES IS A MILD SIDE EFFECT.
HELLO?
hi, is prof. smith there?
uh...
YOU MEAN HERE, IN THE LAB?
yes.
THE ONE WITH HIS NAME ON THE DOOR?
yes.
JORGE CHAM © 2007
THE PLACE WHERE ALL THE WORK HE'LL TAKE CREDIT FOR ACTUALLY GETS DONE?
yes.
YEAH, HE'S NOT HERE RIGHT NOW.
when do you expect him back?
WHEN'S THE NEXT SOLAR ECLIPSE?

NOTHING IS CERTAIN EXCEPT PROCRASTINATION AND TAXES

POP ~~CULTURE~~ CLUELESS

STUFF YOU'VE NO IDEA ABOUT BECAUSE YOU LIVE IN A BUBBLE

How Well Do You Know Your Advisor?

Take the quiz!

1. Where did your advisor go for undergrad? (1 pt.)
2. Where is your advisor's home town? (1 pt.)
3. Who was your advisor's advisor (your grandadvisor)? (1 pt.)
4. How many siblings does he/she have, and what are their professions? (1 pt.)
5. What is your advisor's middle name? (10 pt.)

Your Score:

4-5 - You know WAY too much about your Advisor.

2-3 - You Google-stalked him, didn't you?

0-1 - You have a normal relationship with your Advisor.

(POSTED THE DAY AFTER THE VIRGINIA TECH SHOOTINGS)

THE LAB/OFFICE COUCH

Should you sit in it?

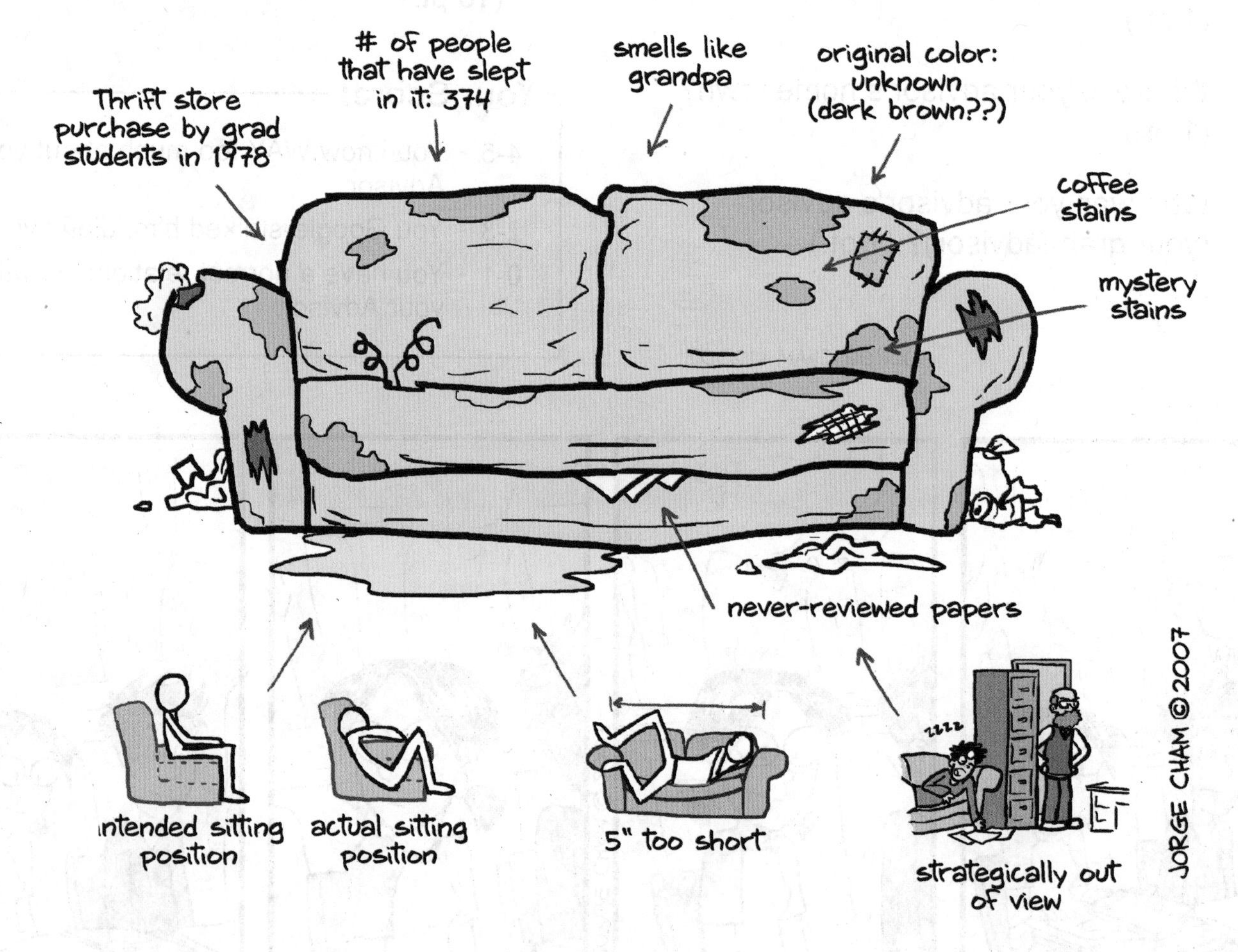

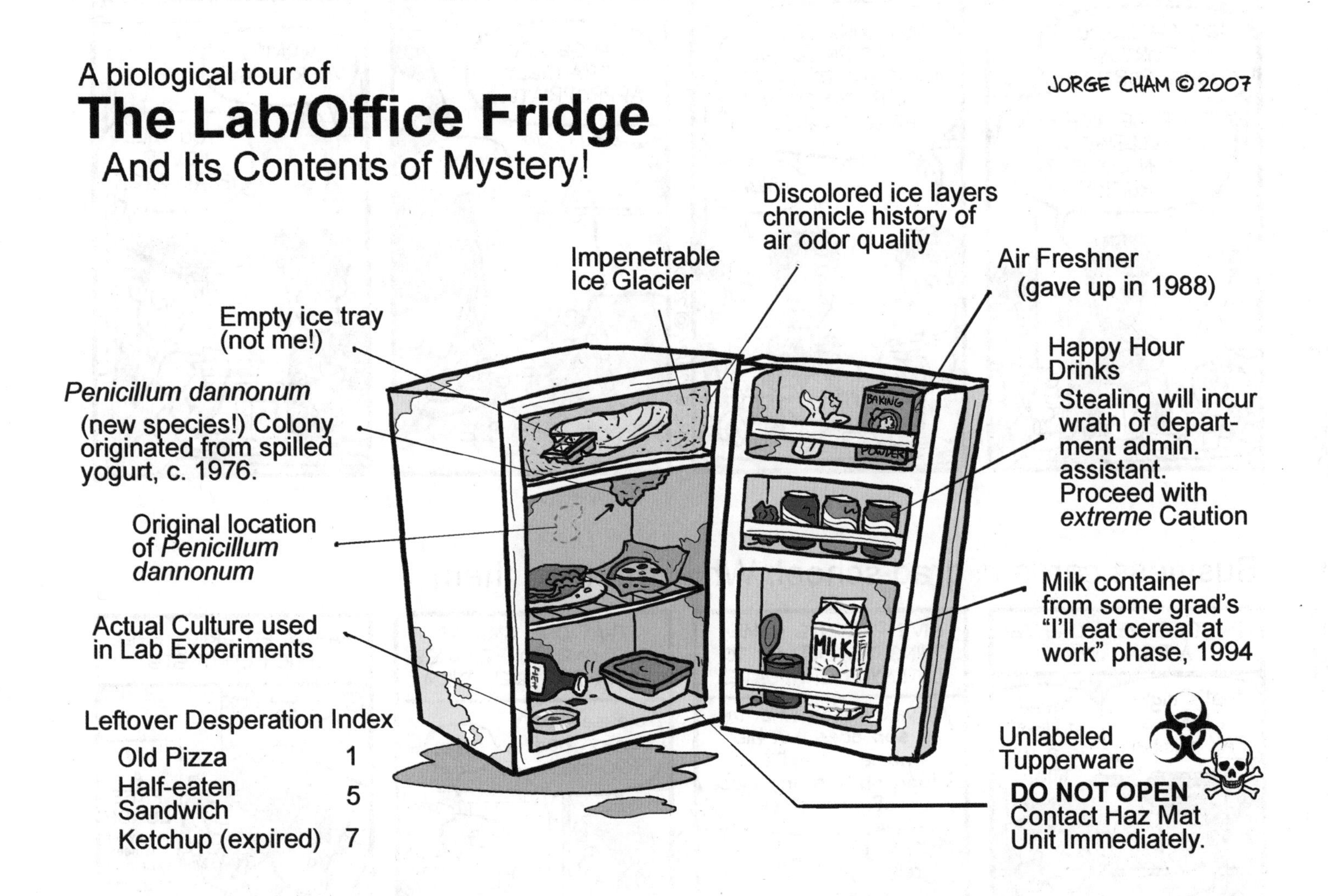
A biological tour of
The Lab/Office Fridge
And Its Contents of Mystery!
JORGE CHAM © 2007
Discolored ice layers chronicle history of air odor quality
Impenetrable Ice Glacier
Air Freshner (gave up in 1988)
Empty ice tray (not me!)
Happy Hour Drinks
Stealing will incur wrath of department admin. assistant. Proceed with extreme Caution
Penicillum dannonum (new species!) Colony originated from spilled yogurt, c. 1976.
Original location of Penicillum dannonum
Milk container from some grad's "I'll eat cereal at work" phase, 1994
Actual Culture used in Lab Experiments
Leftover Desperation Index
Old Pizza 1
Half-eaten Sandwich 5
Ketchup (expired) 7
Unlabeled Tupperware
DO NOT OPEN
Contact Haz Mat Unit Immediately.
BAKING
POWDER
MILK

Business cards in grad school: Why you need them

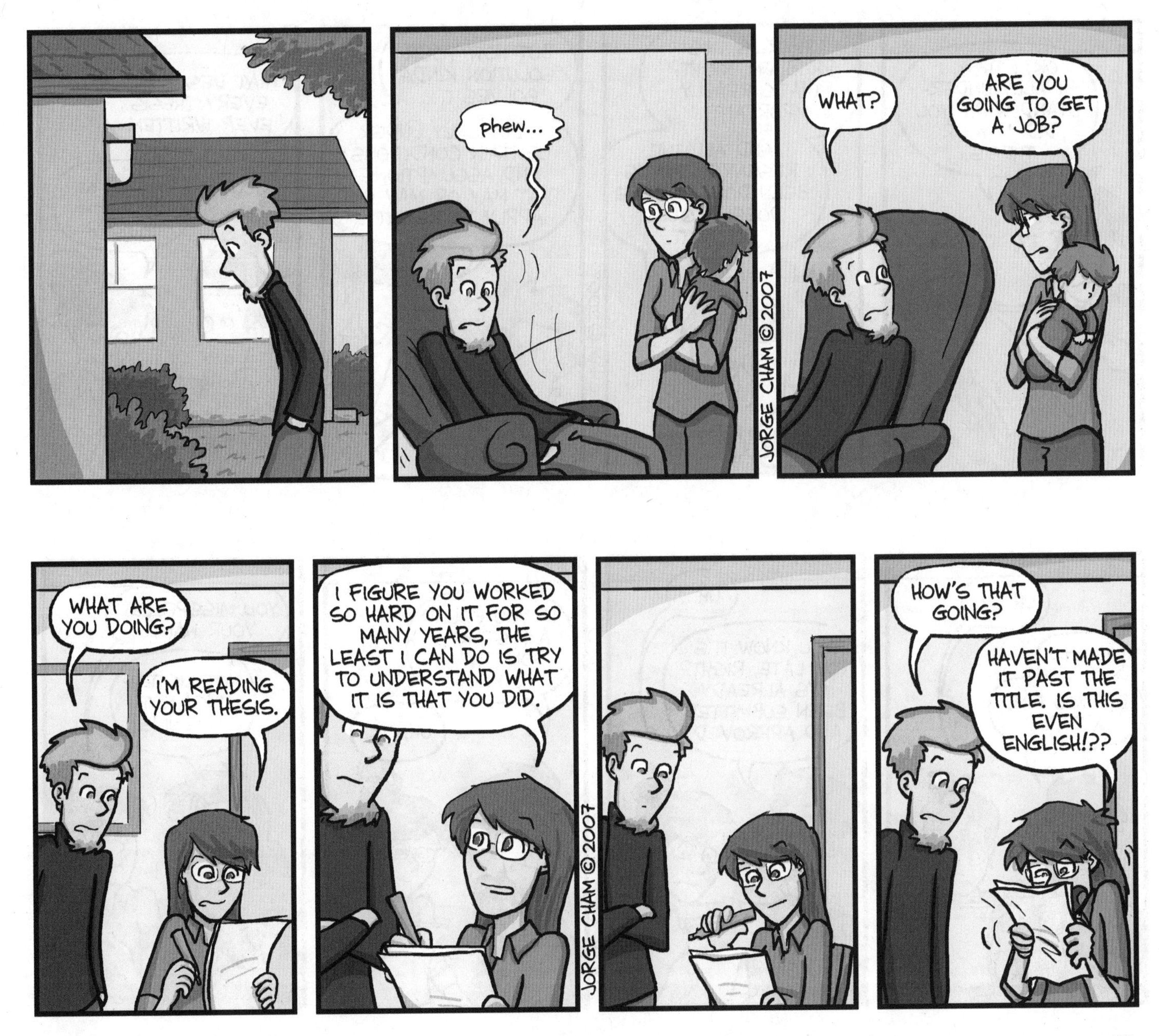
phew...
JORGE CHAM © 2007
WHAT?
ARE YOU GOING TO GET A JOB?
WHAT ARE YOU DOING?
I'M READING YOUR THESIS.
I FIGURE YOU WORKED SO HARD ON IT FOR SO MANY YEARS, THE LEAST I CAN DO IS TRY TO UNDERSTAND WHAT IT IS THAT YOU DID.
JORGE CHAM © 2007
HOW'S THAT GOING?
HAVEN'T MADE IT PAST THE TITLE. IS THIS EVEN ENGLISH!??

OK, I THINK I FINALLY UNDERSTAND WHAT YOU DID IN YOUR THESIS.
THERE'S THIS PROBLEM, RIGHT? THAT'S REALLY IMPORTANT...
AND ALL THE RESEARCH THAT'S BEEN DONE BEFORE DOESN'T QUITE SOLVE IT.
JORGE CHAM © 2007
BUT NOW **YOUR** SOLUTION KINDA SOLVES IT...
...BUT ONLY UNDER CERTAIN CONDITIONS AND ASSUMPTIONS THAT MAY OR MAY NOT APPLY TO REALITY.
THAT DESCRIBES EVERY THESIS EVER WRITTEN.
they all say the same thing??
UH OH.
WHAT?
DID YOU FIND A TYPO?
UH...
YOU KNOW IT'S TOO LATE, RIGHT? IT'S ALREADY BEEN SUBMITTED AND APPROVED.
JORGE CHAM © 2007
IF YOU FOUND A MISTAKE, I DON'T WANT TO KNOW.
UH, OK.
YOU MISSPELLED YOUR NAME.
NOT LISTENING! NOT LISTENING!

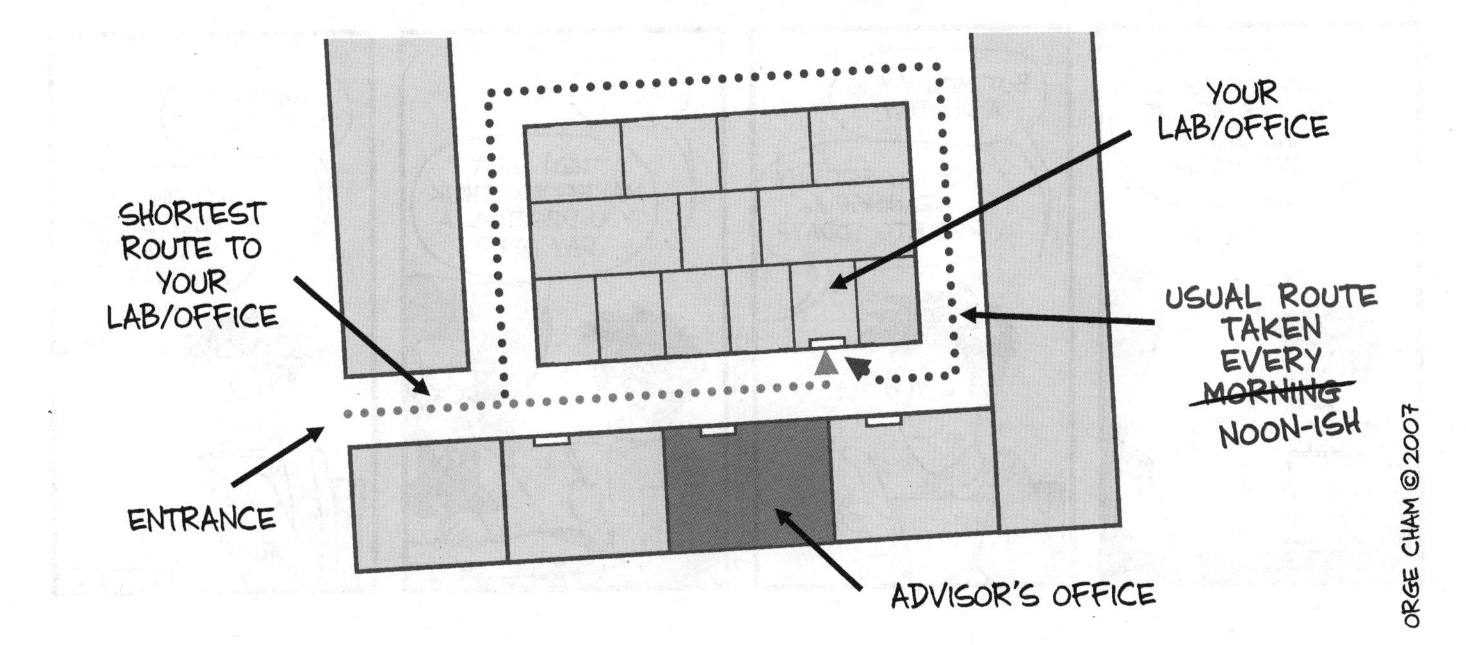

YOUR SHRINKING SENSE OF HUMOR

FROM CHEEKY TO GEEKY IN JUST SEVEN YEARS

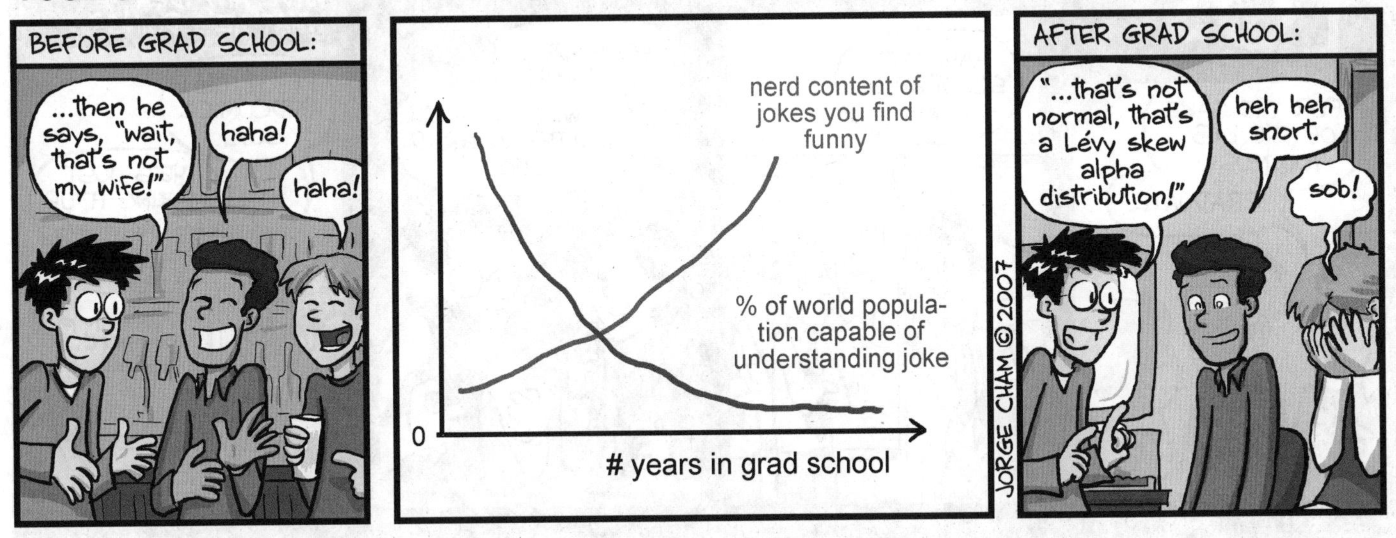

I EXPECT YOU IN THE LAB BRIGHT AND EARLY MONDAY MORNING.
UH...
BUT MONDAY IS A HOLIDAY.
DID YOU GET ANY MEANINGFUL RESULTS TODAY?
JORGE CHAM © 2007
UM, NO.
THEN WHAT MAKES YOU THINK YOU DESERVE A DAY OFF?
THE FACT THAT I TRIED?
YOU ONLY GET POINTS FOR NOT DISAP-POINTING ME.
PREVIOUSLY, ON
LOST
FOR THE SAKE OF THE BABY, YOU MUST...
GRADUATE.
THE "OTHERS"...
AAH! THEY SCOOPED US AGAIN!!
YEARS LATER...
WE MADE A MISTAKE!
IT WAS SO MUCH BETTER IN GRAD SCHOOL!
DOES THE WRITER HAVE ANY IDEA WHAT HE'S DOING?
PFFT! THAT PHDCOMICS GUY...
HE'S JUST MAKING IT UP AS HE GOES.

THERE. I FINISHED YOUR THESIS!
YOU READ THE WHOLE THING?
EVERY WORD. EVEN THE APPENDIX.
JORGE CHAM © 2007
HOW DO YOU FEEL?
NUMB. CONFUSED. NOT REALLY SURE WHY I DID IT. IS THAT NORMAL?
IT'S WHAT GRAD SCHOOL FEELS LIKE. BUT I WOULDN'T CALL IT "NORMAL".
brain... hurts...
SO, ON YOUR THESIS ACKNOWL-EDGMENTS...
YEAH?
YOU THANK YOUR PRO-FESSORS, YOUR PARENTS, YOUR THESIS COMMITTEE, YOUR LABMATES, THE LAB TECH, THE ADMINISTRA-TIVE ASSISTANT, THE I.T. GUY, THE JANITOR, THE CAFETERIA WORKER...
JORGE CHAM © 2007
SO?
DON'T YOU THINK YOU FORGOT SOMEONE? SOMEONE VERY IMPORTANT?
MRS. WONG, MY GRADE SCHOOL TEACHER?
ME! YOUR WIFE?? HELLO??

I DID MENTION YOU IN MY THESIS. IT'S IN THE DEDICATION PAGE.
THERE'S A DEDICATION PAGE?
"JEN AND SOPHY: I LOVE YOU TO PIECES, TO YOU I DEDICATE THIS THESIS..."
JORGE CHAM © 2007
AWW, THAT'S SWEET.
BUT WHY DOES IT LOOK LIKE IT WAS HANDWRITTEN AT THE LAST MINUTE?
IT WAS MORE PERSONAL THAT WAY.
CHECK IT OUT, I PAINTED A PICTURE OF A WINDOW ON OUR WALL.
NOW, WHENEVER YOU GET TIRED OF RESEARCH, YOU CAN JUST LOOK UP!
JORGE CHAM © 2007
I ALSO BOUGHT HELMETS IN CASE ANYONE TRIES TO JUMP OUT.
s-sun-light?

MENU
JORGE CHAM © 2007
LONG DISTANCE RELATIONSHIPS: 1
CECILIA: 0
WHAT RESEARCH HAVE I DONE THIS WEEK?
NONE, WHY?
YOU SEEM A LITTLE DISTRACTED, CECILIA. IS EVERYTHING ALLRIGHT?
UM. SORT OF.
DO YOU WANT TO TALK ABOUT IT?
NOT REALLY.
ARE YOU SURE?
YEAH.
JORGE CHAM © 2007
CECILIA, I HOPE YOU THINK OF ME AS MORE THAN JUST YOUR RESEARCH ADVISOR.
IF YOU NEED ANY KIND OF ADVICE, I WANT YOU TO KNOW I'M HERE FOR YOU.
I BROKE UP WITH MY BOY-FRIEND.
EXCEPT THAT. LET'S GET BACK TO RESEARCH.

IN MY DAY, WE DIDN'T HAVE THE KIND OF PROBLEMS YOU KIDS HAVE TODAY.
IT WAS MUCH SIMPLER BACK THEN. NONE OF THIS MOVING ALL THE TIME, AND HAVING TO DECIDE BETWEEN YOUR CAREER AND YOUR RELATIONSHIPS.
JORGE CHAM © 2007
DID YOUR WIFE MOVE WITH YOU WHEN YOU GOT A FACULTY JOB?
MY FIRST WIFE DID.
YOUR FIRST WIFE?
I WAS A TRIPLE DIVORCÉ BY THE TIME I HAD TENURE.

HHMMMM MMMMMM HMMMMM M
HHMMMM MMMMM
PHD: DOCTOR OF PHOTOCOPYING.
HERE ARE THE COPIES YOU ASKED FOR.
JUST SET IT NEXT TO THAT PILE.
JORGE CHAM © 2007

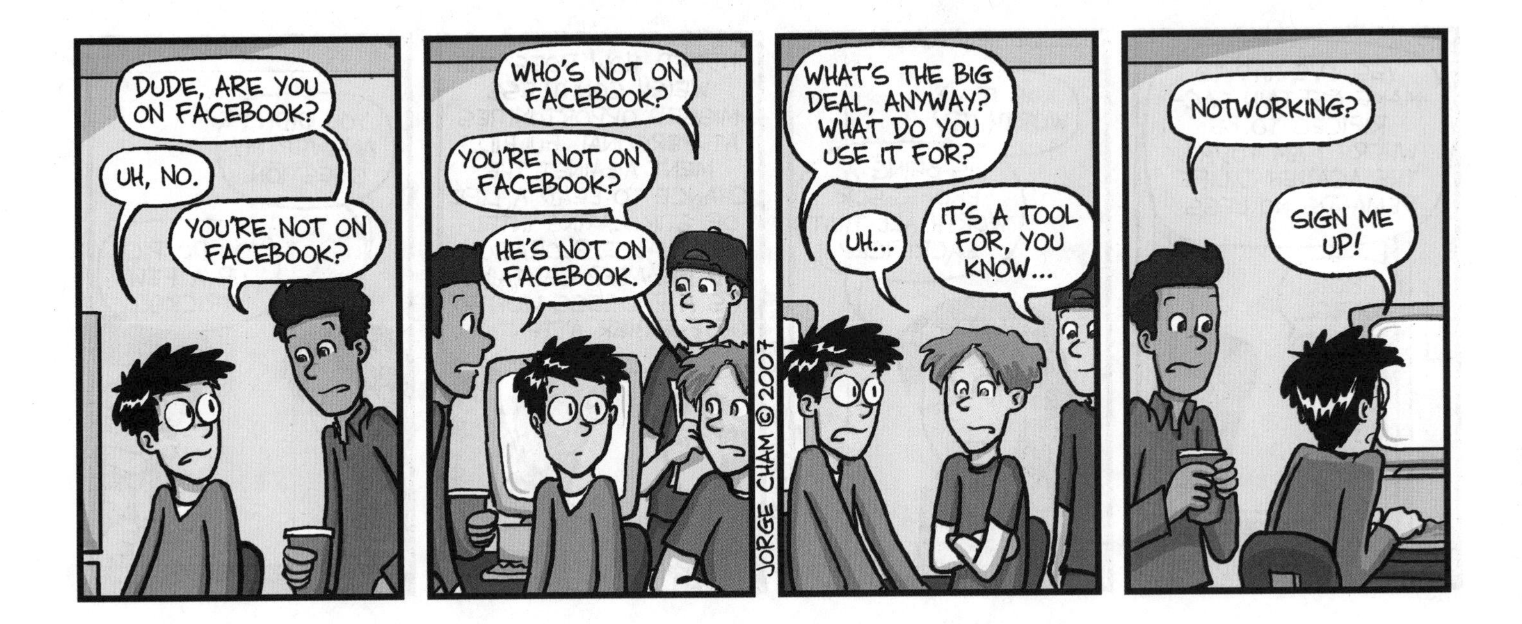
DUDE, ARE YOU ON FACEBOOK?
UH, NO.
YOU'RE NOT ON FACEBOOK?
WHO'S NOT ON FACEBOOK?
YOU'RE NOT ON FACEBOOK?
HE'S NOT ON FACEBOOK.
JORGE CHAM © 2007
WHAT'S THE BIG DEAL, ANYWAY? WHAT DO YOU USE IT FOR?
UH...
IT'S A TOOL FOR, YOU KNOW...
NOTWORKING?
SIGN ME UP!

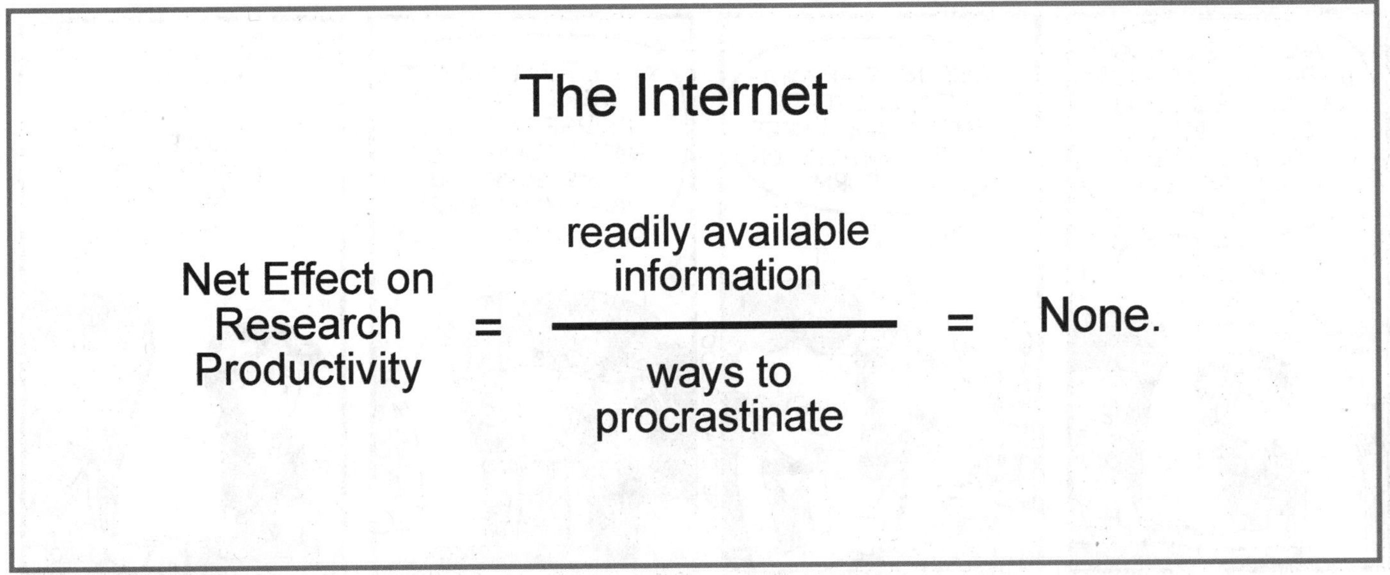
The Internet
Net Effect on Research Productivity
=
readily available information
ways to procrastinate
=
None.

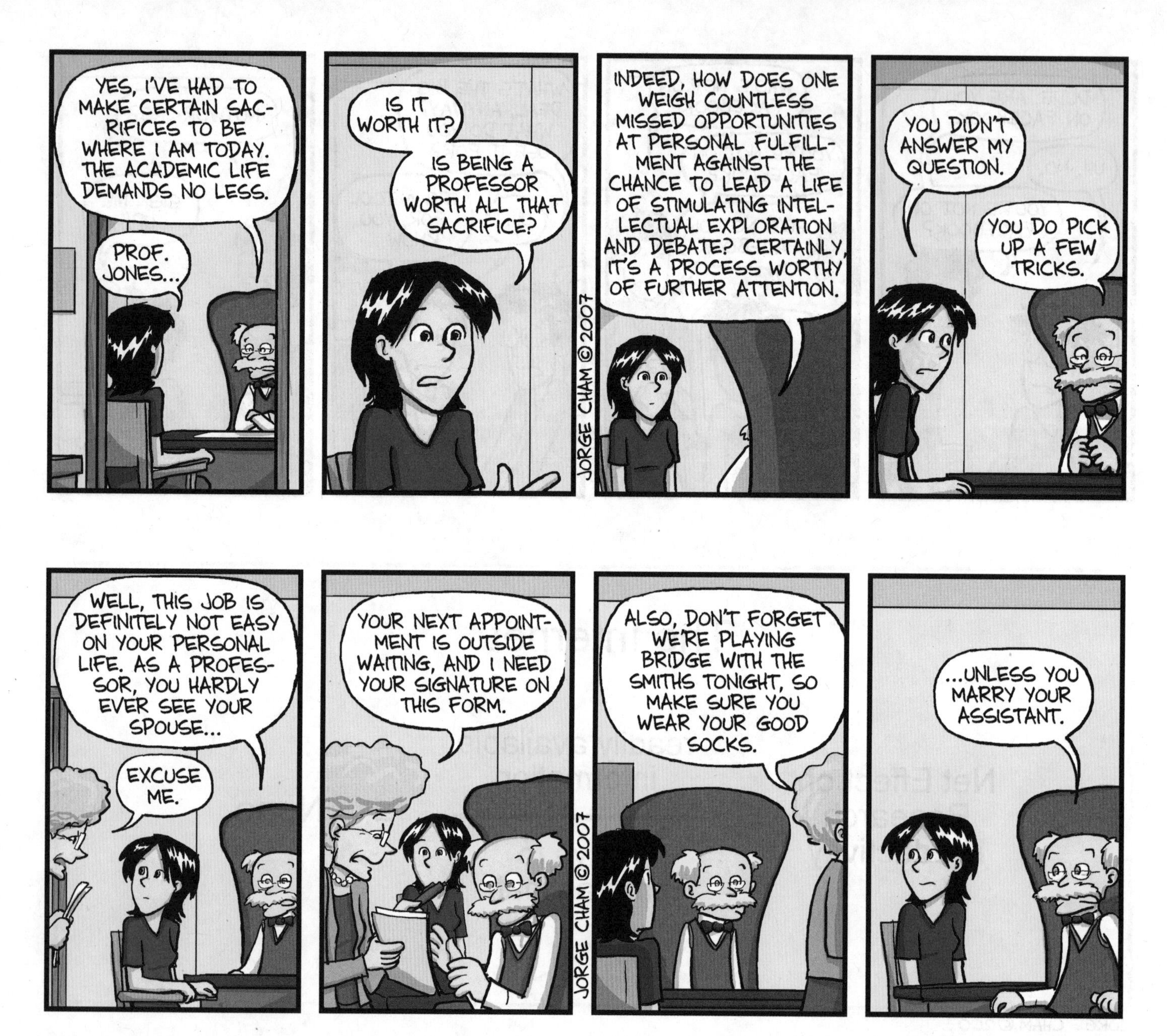
YES, I'VE HAD TO MAKE CERTAIN SACRIFICES TO BE WHERE I AM TODAY. THE ACADEMIC LIFE DEMANDS NO LESS.
PROF. JONES...
IS IT WORTH IT?
IS BEING A PROFESSOR WORTH ALL THAT SACRIFICE?
JORGE CHAM © 2007
INDEED, HOW DOES ONE WEIGH COUNTLESS MISSED OPPORTUNITIES AT PERSONAL FULFILLMENT AGAINST THE CHANCE TO LEAD A LIFE OF STIMULATING INTELLECTUAL EXPLORATION AND DEBATE? CERTAINLY, IT'S A PROCESS WORTHY OF FURTHER ATTENTION.
YOU DIDN'T ANSWER MY QUESTION.
YOU DO PICK UP A FEW TRICKS.
WELL, THIS JOB IS DEFINITELY NOT EASY ON YOUR PERSONAL LIFE. AS A PROFESSOR, YOU HARDLY EVER SEE YOUR SPOUSE...
EXCUSE ME.
YOUR NEXT APPOINTMENT IS OUTSIDE WAITING, AND I NEED YOUR SIGNATURE ON THIS FORM.
JORGE CHAM © 2007
ALSO, DON'T FORGET WE'RE PLAYING BRIDGE WITH THE SMITHS TONIGHT, SO MAKE SURE YOU WEAR YOUR GOOD SOCKS.
...UNLESS YOU MARRY YOUR ASSISTANT.

HEY, MIKE, WE'RE-
AH. AH. PLEASE. IT'S DR. SLACK-ENERNY.
NOW THAT I SUBMITTED MY THESIS, I HAVE ENTERED A NEW LEVEL OF ACADEMIC RESPECTABILITY AND DECORUM.
JORGE CHAM © 2007
THERE IS A DEGREE OF FORMALITY AND DIGNIFIED BEHAVIOR THAT I EXPECT OF MYSELF AND OTHERS FROM NOW ON.
THERE'S FREE FOOD DOWN IN THE LOBBY.
DOCTORS FIRST.
I SHOULD GET BACK TO THE LAB.
JORGE CHAM © 2007

HEY, CECILIA.
HEY...
UH, ARE YOU OK?
YEAH...
JORGE CHAM © 2007
CECILIA, YOU'RE NOT GOING TO BELIEVE THIS, BUT SOMEBODY'S GIVING AWAY FREE CHOCOLATE OUTSIDE!
FREE CHOCOLATE!
MEH.
I'LL PASS.
UH OH!
STILL SAD ABOUT THE LONG DISTANCE BREAK-UP?
YEAH...
I'M TRYING TO GET BACK TO WORK, BUT... WHAT'S THE POINT?
JORGE CHAM © 2007
sigh.
sniff.
WHEN WAS THE LAST TIME YOU SHOWERED?
WHAT'S THE POINT OF ANYTHING??

PROCRASTINATION = MIND / MATTER
PROCRASTINATION × MATTER = MIND
MATTER = MIND / PROCRASTINATION
→ IF MIND = Ø
∴ MATTER = Ø / PROCRASTINATION = Ø
JORGE CHAM © 2007
PROCRASTNATION: IF NOBODY MINDS, IT DOESN'T REALLY MATTER.
HUH.

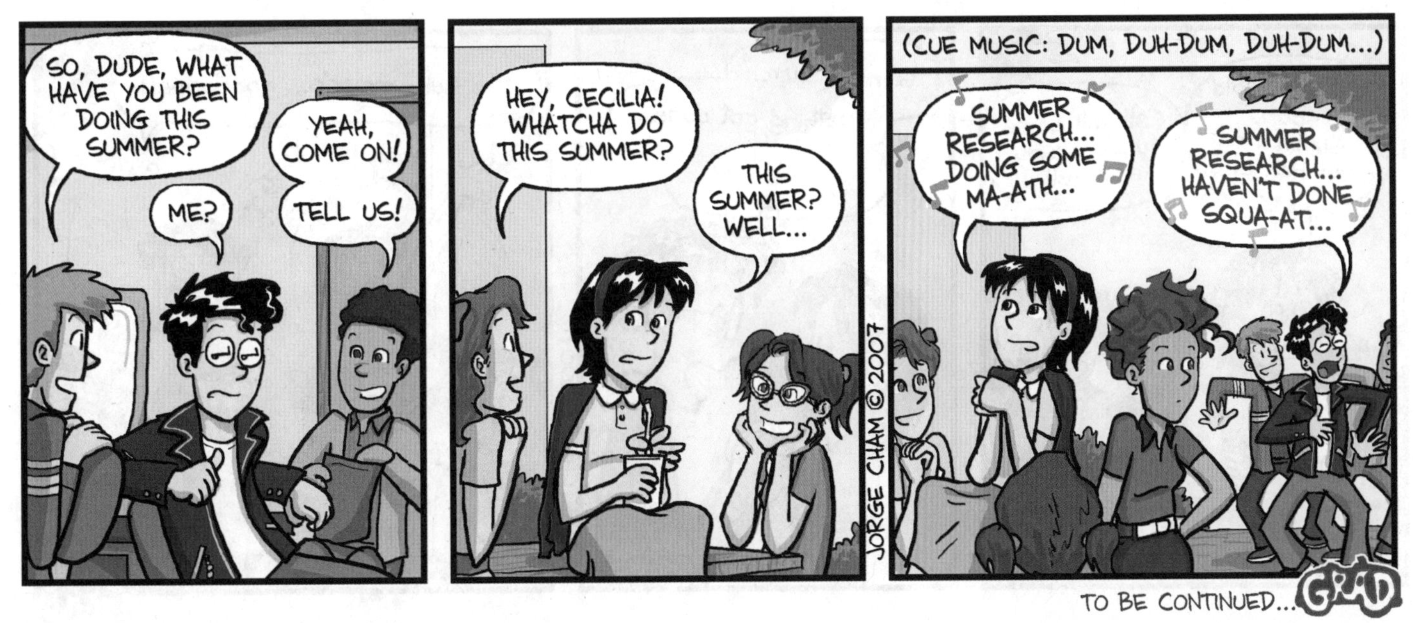
SO, DUDE, WHAT HAVE YOU BEEN DOING THIS SUMMER?
YEAH, COME ON!
ME?
TELL US!
HEY, CECILIA! WHATCHA DO THIS SUMMER?
THIS SUMMER? WELL...
JORGE CHAM © 2007
(CUE MUSIC: DUM, DUH-DUM, DUH-DUM...)
SUMMER RESEARCH... DOING SOME MA-ATH...
SUMMER RESEARCH... HAVEN'T DONE SQUA-AT...
TO BE CONTINUED...
GRAD

wrote some code, it's still in beta...
goofed around, don't got no data!
summer days, toiling away...
in that uh-oh suh-ummer daze!
JORGE CHAM © 2007
well-ah-well-ah-well-ah...
tell me more, tell me more...
didja make any graphs?
tell me more, tell me more...
did your prof. have a laugh?
yeah.
It'll turn cold soon, Summer's been heh-ell...
Fall will come, undergrads smeh-ell..!
Summer bum...
nothing got done...
And now... oh...
JORGE CHAM © 2007
The Suh-ummer's... gooooone!!
Back to work...
back to work..!
GRAD

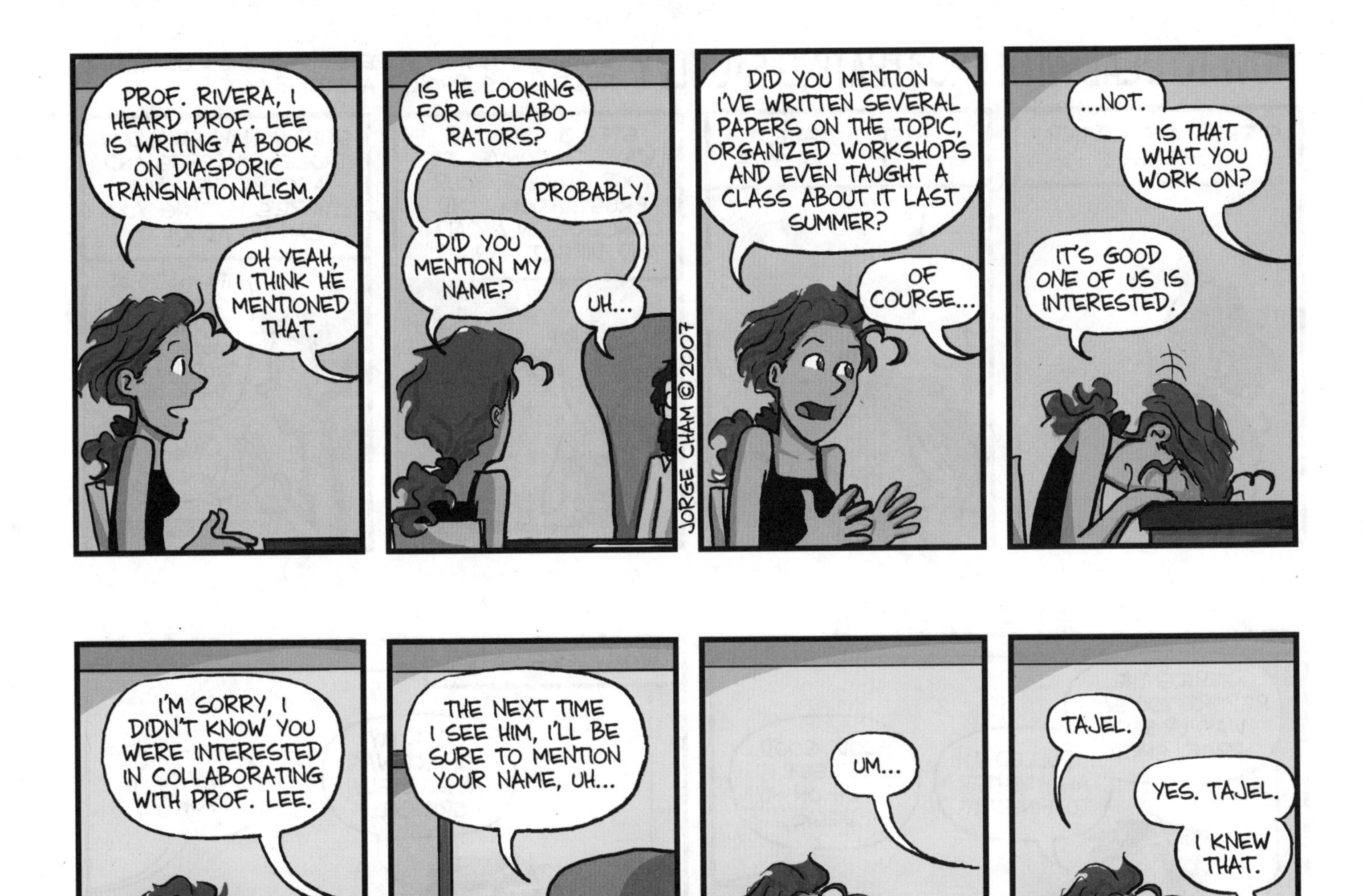
PROF. RIVERA, I HEARD PROF. LEE IS WRITING A BOOK ON DIASPORIC TRANSNATIONALISM.
OH YEAH, I THINK HE MENTIONED THAT.
IS HE LOOKING FOR COLLABO-RATORS?
PROBABLY.
DID YOU MENTION MY NAME?
UH...
JORGE CHAM © 2007
DID YOU MENTION I'VE WRITTEN SEVERAL PAPERS ON THE TOPIC, ORGANIZED WORKSHOPS AND EVEN TAUGHT A CLASS ABOUT IT LAST SUMMER?
OF COURSE...
...NOT.
IS THAT WHAT YOU WORK ON?
IT'S GOOD ONE OF US IS INTERESTED.
I'M SORRY, I DIDN'T KNOW YOU WERE INTERESTED IN COLLABORATING WITH PROF. LEE.
THE NEXT TIME I SEE HIM, I'LL BE SURE TO MENTION YOUR NAME, UH...
JORGE CHAM © 2007
UM...
TAJEL.
YES. TAJEL.
I KNEW THAT.

HOW TO DEAL WITH FRUSTRATING FACULTY

EXASPERATED BY A PERCEIVED LACK OF INTEREST AND SUPPORT? A STEP-BY-STEP GUIDE:

THE "3 TIMES" RULE

Always wait ***three times*** *before doing something your advisor asks you to do.*

AVOID GETTING BURIED IN POINTLESS AND UNNECESSARY TASKS TO THE DETRIMENT OF PRODUCTIVE ~~WEB SURFING~~ WORK

BE REASONABLE, SMITH. HIS PROJECT IS BRINGING IN 13 MILLION DOLLARS. IF YOU'RE NOT USING THE SPACE-
I AM TOO!
OH, REALLY?
IS THIS WHAT YOU CALL "RESEARCH"?
WHY, YOU INSOLENT..!
Evidence A - Room #0157
Smith Lab "Annex"
JORGE CHAM © 2007
I WAS WRITING GRANTS BEFORE YOU WERE BORN!
GENTLEMEN, PLEASE-!
AGHHH!
DIPLOMACY FAILS.

ALLRIGHT, MEN, LISTEN UP.
AHEM.
YOU TOO, ALLISON.
WE ARE AT WAR.
JORGE CHAM © 2007
THE FORCES OF TYRANNY (I.E. THE DEPARTMENT CHAIR) WANT TO TAKE AWAY OUR "UNDER-UTILIZED" RESOURCES, BUT I SAY UNTO THEM...
GIVE ME LAB SPACE... OR GIVE ME DEATH!
DEATH?
OR A BIGGER OFFICE.

ONE DAY YOU WILL LOOK UPON TODAY AND REMEMBER THAT WE STOOD FOR SOMETHING, FOR OUR ACTIONS WILL ECHO IN ETERNITY.
WE WILL FIGHT THEM IN THE HALLS, WE WILL FIGHT THEM IN THE CONFERENCE ROOMS. WE SHALL NOT FLAG OR FAIL, WE SHALL NEVER SURRENDER!!
JORGE CHAM © 2007
AND BY "WE" YOU MEAN..?
YOU, YES. AND FETCH ME SOME COFFEE.

THEY'RE HERE!
ALLRIGHT, MEN, MOVE OUT!
UH...
YOU TOO ALLISON.
THANK-YOU.
JORGE CHAM © 2007
THE FIGHTING BEGINS!
EXCUSE ME, ARE YOU USING THIS LAB BENCH?
YES!
OH, YEAH? THEN WHAT DOES THIS EQUIPMENT DO?
UH...
MAN DOWN! MAN DOWN!

WE CAN'T HOLD THEM, SIR!
THERE'S ONLY SO MUCH LAB SPACE WE CAN PRETEND TO USE AT THE SAME TIME!
JORGE CHAM © 2007
CURSES!
WHAT'S THE CASUALTY REPORT?
IT'S JIMMY, SIR, THE SUMMER INTERN... HE'S...
HE'S...
...HE JOINED THE OTHER LAB.
HE WAS MY LACKEY!
THIS MAY WORK TO OUR ADVANTAGE. SUMMER INTERNS ARE USELESS.

THEY'VE TAKEN OVER THE WATER COOLER SIR! THEY'RE ALMOST AT THE MAIN LAB!
DARN IT, IF ONLY MY RESEARCH USED TRENDIER BUZZWORDS!
WE'LL HAVE TO BARRICADE THE COPIER ROOM. THAT'S WHERE WE'LL MAKE OUR LAST STAND..!
JORGE CHAM © 2007
IF WE SHOULD FALL TODAY, GENTLEMEN, I WANT YOU TO KNOW THAT HAVING YOU WORK FOR ME HAS BEEN A TRUE HONOR...
...FOR YOU.
NOT MANY PEOPLE GET THAT PRIVILEGE.
HERE THEY COME!

THERE WE WERE: CORNERED, HOPELESSLY OUT-NUMBERED AND OUT-FUNDED... THE FATE OF OUR LAB NEARLY LOST.
WHEN SUDDENLY, A MIRACLE OCCURRED...
JORGE CHAM © 2007
YOU MANAGED TO FIGHT THEM OFF?
THE DEAN GAVE THEM STATE-OF-THE-ART FACILITIES IN A BRAND NEW BUILDING, SO THEY LEFT.
WELL, I HOPE YOU KIDS APPRECIATE THE SACRIFICES WE MADE TO SECURE THE LAB SPACE YOU TAKE FOR GRANTED.
NOT A DAY GOES BY I DON'T WONDER WHERE ANY OF US WOULD BE IF WE HAD LOST THAT DAY...
JORGE CHAM © 2007
I WOULDN'T STILL BE IN GRAD SCHOOL, FOR EXAMPLE.
HEY, OLD MAN, BACK TO WORK OR YOU'LL NEVER GRADUATE!
ALLRIGHT! ALLRIGHT!
Here were fought the Territorial Disputes of 2007
Wherein many young men (and one woman) lost their leisure for a cause greater than themselves: their Advisor.

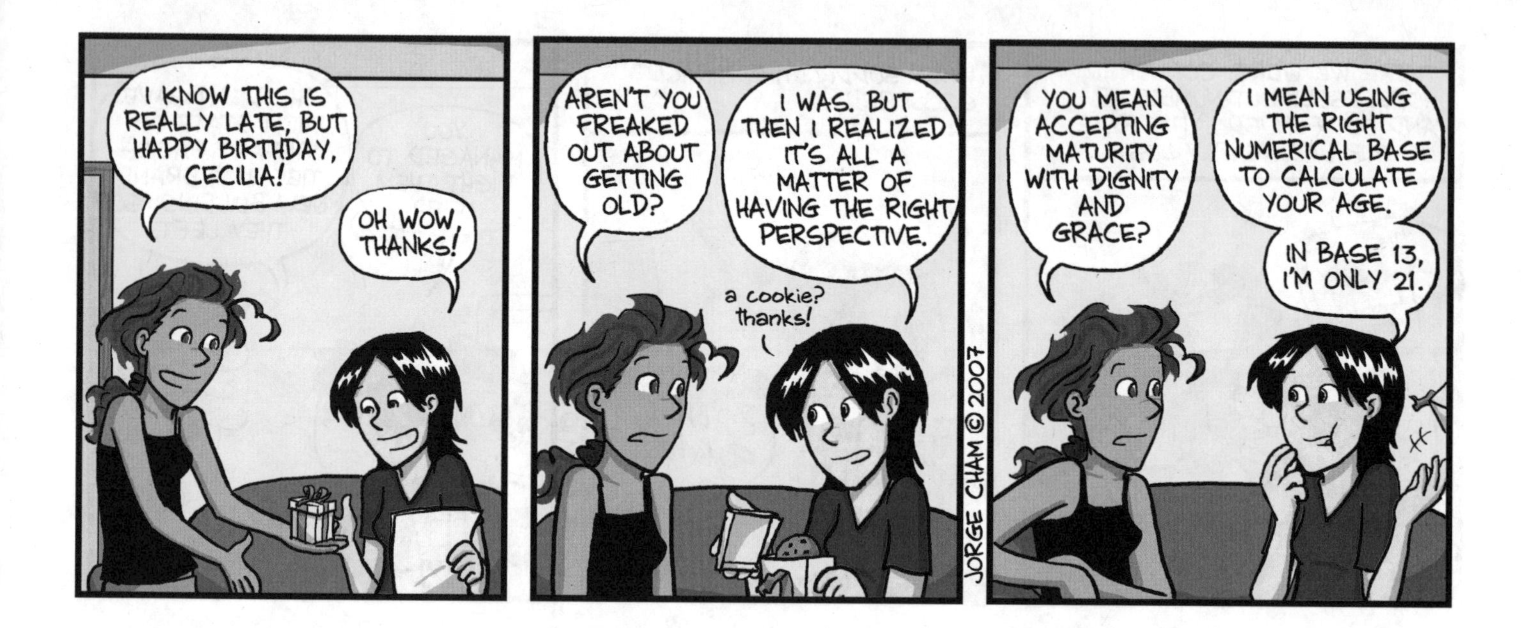

I KNOW THIS IS REALLY LATE, BUT HAPPY BIRTHDAY, CECILIA!
OH WOW, THANKS!
AREN'T YOU FREAKED OUT ABOUT GETTING OLD?
I WAS. BUT THEN I REALIZED IT'S ALL A MATTER OF HAVING THE RIGHT PERSPECTIVE.
a cookie? thanks!
JORGE CHAM © 2007
YOU MEAN ACCEPTING MATURITY WITH DIGNITY AND GRACE?
I MEAN USING THE RIGHT NUMERICAL BASE TO CALCULATE YOUR AGE.
IN BASE 13, I'M ONLY 21.

WHOA, WHEN DID WE GET A LASER??
HUH. MUST BE A NEW PROJECT.
WARNING
LASER IN USE!
DO NOT ENTER!
JORGE CHAM © 2007
SOUNDS DANGEROUS. WE BETTER STAY CLEAR.
WASN'T THERE A CLOSET HERE BEFORE?
ZZZZZ!

ANOVA: ANALYSIS OF VALUE

IS YOUR RESEARCH WORTH ANYTHING?

Developed in 1912 by geneticist R.A. Fisher, the Analysis of Value is a powerful statistical tool designed to test the significance of one's work.

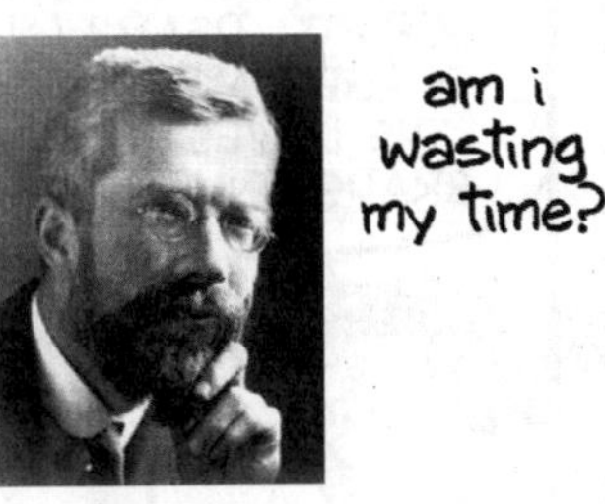

am i wasting my time?

Significance is determined by comparing one's research with the **Dull Hypothesis**:

$$H_o : \mu_1 = \mu_2 \ ?$$

where,

H_o : the Dull Hypothesis

μ_1 : significance of your research

μ_2 : significance of a monkey typing randomly on a typewriter in a forest where no one hears it.

The test involves computation of the *F'd* ratio:

$$F'd = \frac{\text{sum(people who care about your research)}}{\text{world population}}$$

This ratio is compared to the F distribution with I-1, N_T degrees of freedom to determine a *p(in your pants)* value. A low *p(in your pants)* value means you're on to something good (though statistically improbable).

Type I/II Errors

The Analysis of Value must be used carefully to avoid the following two types of errors:

Type I: You incorrectly believe your research is not Dull.

Type II: No conclusions can be made. Good luck graduating.

Of course, this test assumes both Independence and Normality on your part, neither of which is likely true, which means *it's not your problem.*

OVER THE YEARS, WE'VE RECEIVED MANY LETTERS LIKE THIS ONE:
Please! We in the Humanities need our own Ph.D character. (preferably in German Literature). Kyle & Florence
WELL, FEEL IGNORED NO MORE, HUMANITIES MAJORS! I AM HAPPY TO INTRODUCE OUR NEWEST CHARACTER, GERARD!
HELLO.
JORGE CHAM © 2007
GERARD IS A MEDIEVAL SCANDINAVIAN CULTURAL PHILOSOPHY MAJOR, SO YOU CAN BE SURE THERE'LL BE PLENTY OF JOKES ABOUT OBSCURE MANUSCRIPTS, DEAD LANGUAGES AND BEING THE LOWEST PAID GRADS ON CAMPUS!
UM, WE PREFER THE TERM "MONETARILY CHALLENGED."
ALSO: POLITICAL CORRECTNESS!
GERARD, MANY OF OUR READERS ARE NOT FAMILIAR WITH THE DIFFERENCE BETWEEN THE HUMANITIES AND SOCIAL SCIENCES.
LET US ELABORATE!
HUMANITIES IS THE STUDY OF THE HUMAN CONDITION THROUGH LITERARY ANALYSIS AND CRITICISM.
...WHILE US SOCIAL SCIENTISTS USE REAL DATA.
JORGE CHAM © 2007
YOU CALL SUBJECTIVE "INTERVIEWS" AND "LIFE HISTORIES" "REAL DATA"?
WHATEVER. AT LEAST WE DON'T "MAKE STUFF UP."
SPECULATIVE ANALYSIS IS NOT "MAKING STUFF UP"!
look at me! i sit in a room with some books! give me a PHD!

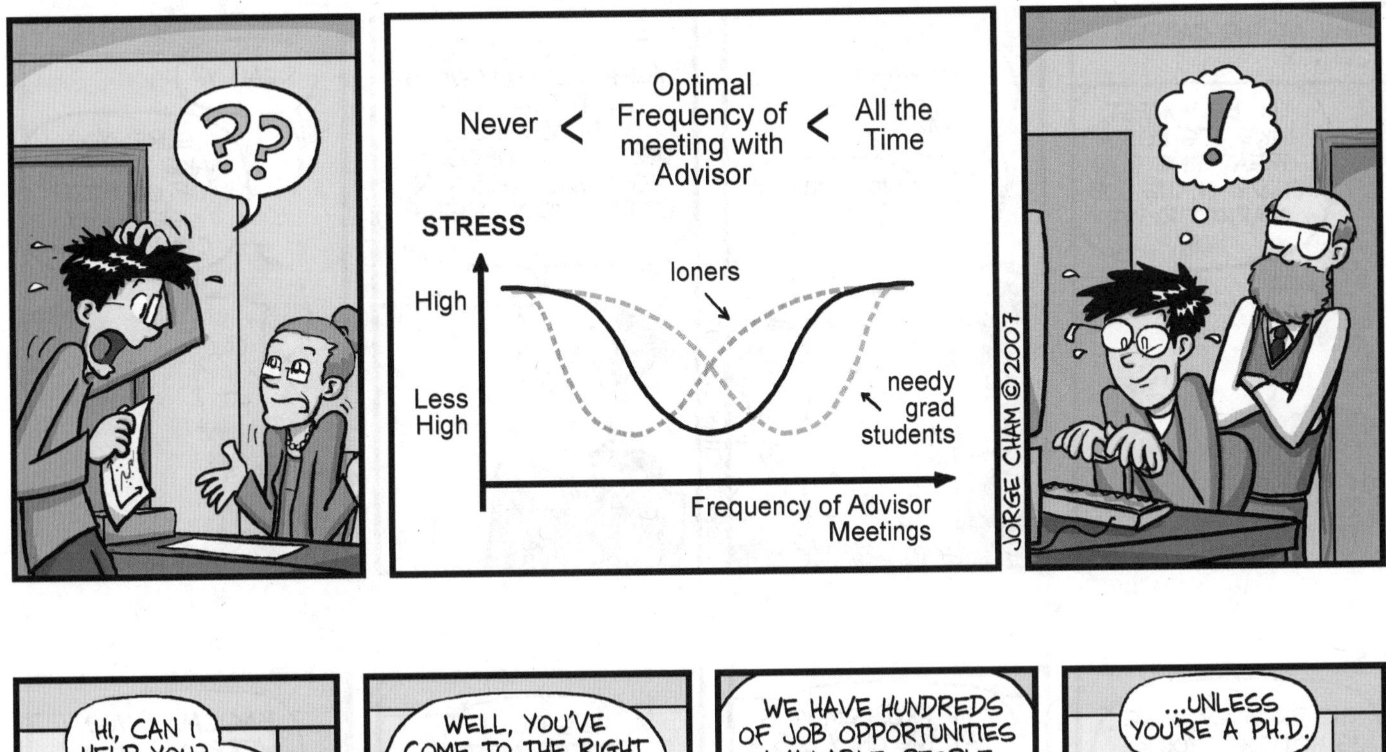
??
Never < Optimal Frequency of meeting with Advisor < All the Time
STRESS
High
Less High
loners
needy grad students
Frequency of Advisor Meetings
JORGE CHAM © 2007
!

HI, CAN I HELP YOU?
UH, YEAH, I NEED A JOB. A REAL ONE?
WELL, YOU'VE COME TO THE RIGHT PLACE! WELCOME TO THE CAREER SERVICES CENTER!
JORGE CHAM © 2007
WE HAVE HUNDREDS OF JOB OPPORTUNITIES AVAILABLE. PEOPLE ARE LITERALLY THROWING THEMSELVES TO HIRE GRADUATES OF THIS UNIVERSITY...
...UNLESS YOU'RE A PH.D.
UH...
COMPUTER SCIENCE?
ACTUALLY-
SORRY, WE'RE CLOSED.
SLAM!

MIKE AT THE CAREER CENTER:
I'LL BE HONEST, MIKE, IT'S NOT A GREAT TIME FOR PH.D.s IN THE JOB MARKET RIGHT NOW.
WHEN WAS IT A GOOD TIME?
WELL, THERE WAS LESS COMPETITION IN 1861.
JORGE CHAM © 2007
BUT DON'T WORRY. THERE WILL ALWAYS BE A NEED FOR PEOPLE WITH ADVANCED DEGREES IN OBSCURE, ESOTERIC FIELDS OF STUDY LIKE YOURSELF.
REALLY?
SURE, YOU MAKE THE REST OF US FEEL USEFUL BY COMPARISON.
THE PROBLEM, MIKE, IS NOT THAT YOU'RE OVERQUALIFIED FOR MOST OF THE JOBS OUT THERE...
THE PROBLEM IS THAT THE ONLY JOB YOU ARE QUALIFIED FOR IS ALREADY TAKEN... BY YOUR ADVISOR.
JORGE CHAM © 2007
HE'S MUCH BETTER AT IT THAN YOU ARE.
AND HE'S NEVER GOING TO RETIRE.
BASICALLY, YOU WERE OUT OF A JOB BEFORE YOU STARTED.
GREAT. I HAVE A PH.D. IN OBSOLESCENCE.

GOODBYE SUMMER

GUYS, I APPRECIATE YOU ALL COMING OUT, BUT DON'T YOU SEE?
WE DON'T NEED A CHARACTER FOR EVERY MAJOR. WE'RE ALL IN THIS TOGETHER! MY STRUGGLE IS YOUR STRUGGLE. THE GRAD SCHOOL EXPERIENCE IS UNIVERSAL!
JORGE CHAM © 2007
ALSO, IT'S NOT A PAYING POSITION.
WELL, GOTTA GO.
SEE YA.
i'll stay!
I WANT THIS PROJECT FINISHED BY NEXT WEEK.
NEXT WEEK?
UH...
IF I TELL HIM HOW IMPOSSIBLE IT IS TO FINISH BY NEXT WEEK, HE'LL THINK I'M INCOMPETENT.
JORGE CHAM © 2007
BUT IF I COMPLAIN OF ALL THE ALL-NIGHTERS I'LL HAVE TO PULL TO ACTUALLY DO IT, HE'LL THINK I'M NOT COMMITTED TO THE PROJECT.
SURE, NO PROBLEM.
HMM, SOUNDS LIKE YOU DON'T HAVE ENOUGH TO DO. CAN YOU ALSO...

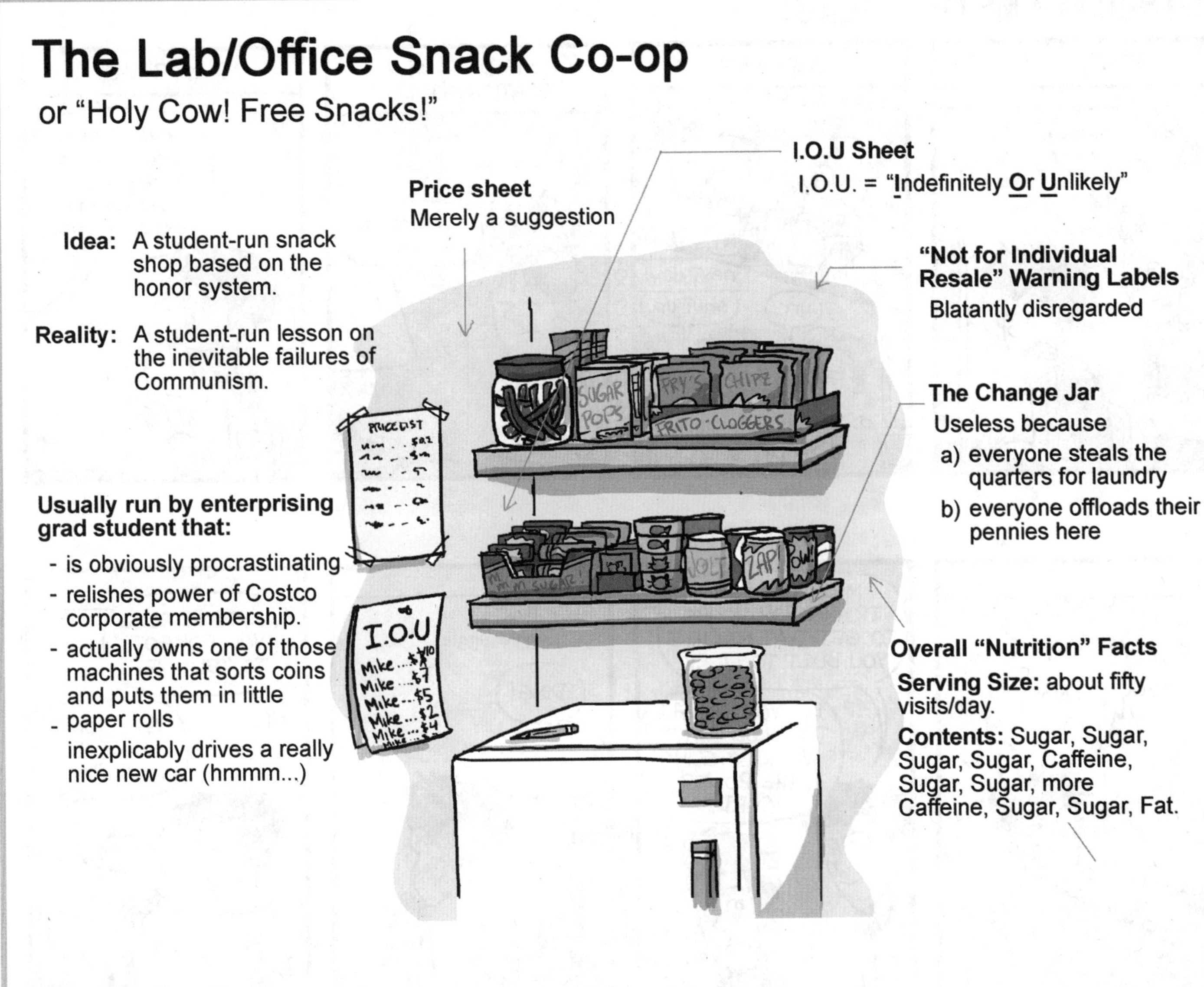
The Lab/Office Snack Co-op
or "Holy Cow! Free Snacks!"
Idea: A student-run snack shop based on the honor system.
Reality: A student-run lesson on the inevitable failures of Communism.
Usually run by enterprising grad student that:
- is obviously procrastinating
- relishes power of Costco corporate membership.
- actually owns one of those machines that sorts coins and puts them in little paper rolls
- inexplicably drives a really nice new car (hmmm...)
Price sheet
Merely a suggestion
I.O.U Sheet
I.O.U. = "Indefinitely Or Unlikely"
"Not for Individual Resale" Warning Labels
Blatantly disregarded
The Change Jar
Useless because
a) everyone steals the quarters for laundry
b) everyone offloads their pennies here
Overall "Nutrition" Facts
Serving Size: about fifty visits/day.
Contents: Sugar, Sugar, Sugar, Sugar, Caffeine, Sugar, Sugar, more Caffeine, Sugar, Sugar, Fat.
SUGAR POPS
FRY'S
CHIPZ
FRITO-CLOGGERS
VOLT
ZAP!
OW!
I.O.U
Mike...$7
Mike...$5
Mike...$2
Mike...$4
JORGE CHAM © 2007

OTHER FORMS OF JETLAG:

YOUR THESIS MUST BE AN ORIGINAL PIECE OF WORK.
...BUT NOT TOO ORIGINAL I CAN'T MAKE SURE YOU DON'T EMBARRASS ME.
JORGE CHAM © 2007
IT MUST BE NEW AND GROUND BREAKING, YET FOLLOW THE SAME VISION AND PROTO-COLS I ESTABLISHED DECADES AGO.
SO, WHEN YOU SAY ORIGINAL, YOU ACTUALLY MEAN..?
MORE OF THE SAME. BUT DIFFERENT.
CHECK IT OUT, I'VE BEEN ASKED TO BE A PAPER REVIEWER FOR NEXT YEAR'S CONFERENCE.
WHOA.
I GUESS THEY CONSIDER ME AN EXPERT IN THE FIELD.
REALLY? WHAT WAS YOUR QUALIFICATION?
JORGE CHAM © 2007
UH, I HAD A PAPER PUBLISHED IN THE SAME CONFERENCE THE YEAR BEFORE.
BUT THAT MEANS YOUR PAPER WAS REVIEWED...
...BY PEOPLE WHOSE ONLY QUALIFICATION WAS TO BE REVIEWED BY THE PREVIOUS YEAR'S PEOPLE WHOSE ONLY QUALIFICATION WAS...
STOP, YOU'RE MAKING MY EGO HURT!

WELL, I'M OFF TO MY T.A. RECITATION SESSION.
I PREPARED LECTURE NOTES AND HANDOUTS WITH EXTRA PROBLEMS, A SPECIAL TUTORIAL FOR THE HOMEWORK AND I PRE-REHEARSED THE EXAMPLES I'M GOING TO WORK OUT IN CLASS TODAY.
JORGE CHAM © 2007
WOW, I REALLY HOPE THEY APPRECIATE ALL YOUR WORK.
OH, SURE...
...IF THEY BOTHERED TO SHOW UP.
QUESTIONS? ANYONE?
ZZZZ
WHY DOESN'T ANYONE COME TO MY T.A. SESSION? WHERE'S THE REST OF THE CLASS?
UH...
IS THIS A BAD TIME? IS THE ROOM HARD TO FIND?
JORGE CHAM © 2007
IS THERE ANOTHER EVENT ON CAMPUS AT THE SAME TIME?
BECAUSE THE ONLY OTHER EXPLANATION IS... IS...
...THAT I'M A BAD T.A.!!
IS THIS GOING TO BE ON THE TEST?

IS THAT WHY NOBODY COMES TO MY T.A. SESSIONS?
AM I THAT BORING?
AM I A TOTAL FAILURE AT INSPIRING YOU TO LEARN?
JORGE CHAM © 2007
UH...
IT'S NOT YOU, IT'S US?
GREAT. LIKE I HAVEN'T HEARD THAT BEFORE.
Re: Fall Break
Grad students are reminded they are expected to work through the Fall Semester Break. -the Dept. Head
but i already bought tickets to go home!
THE FIRST YEAR RESPONSE.
great. more time to work.
THE THIRD YEAR RESPONSE.
JORGE CHAM © 2007
it's fall already? i thought it was july!
THE FIFTH YEAR RESPONSE.
(cricket sounds)
THE MIKE SLACKENERNY RESPONSE.

Oh no, your paper exceeds the maximum number of pages allowed! What do you do??

TIPS AND TRICKS
FOR KEEPING YOUR PAPER WITHIN THE PAGE LIMIT

Shrink font size to limits of human perception

If a minimum font sized is imposed, use a font that is 0.2pt smaller. They won't notice, will they?

Take out excessive details of your methodology

Let's face it, nobody really cares (and if they do, why help your competition?)

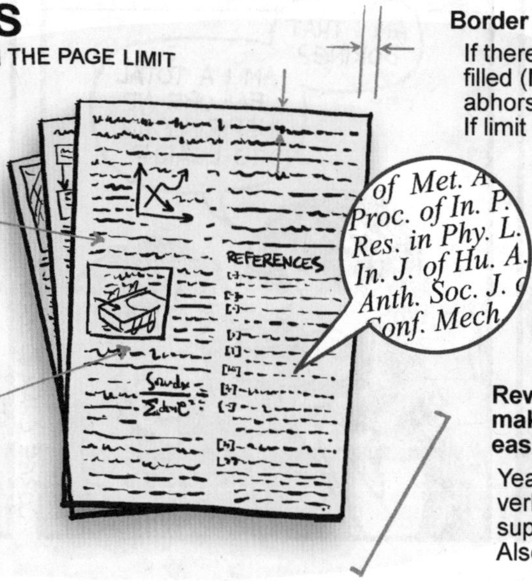

REFERENCES

of Met. A
Proc. of In. P.
Res. in Phy. L.
In. J. of Hu. A.
Anth. Soc. J.
Conf. Mech.

Border size Rule-of-thumb:

If there is paper exposed, it can be filled (Nature, and other journals, abhors a vacuous submission). If limit exists, apply 0.2pt rule.

Use Max. Abbrev. in Ref. Sec.

Spelling out the journal names will only make it easy for people to look up your competitors' papers.

Rewrite entire paper to make it more concise and easier to understand

Yeah right. Prodigious verbiage establishes your superior intelligence. Also, who has the time?

JORGE CHAM © 2007

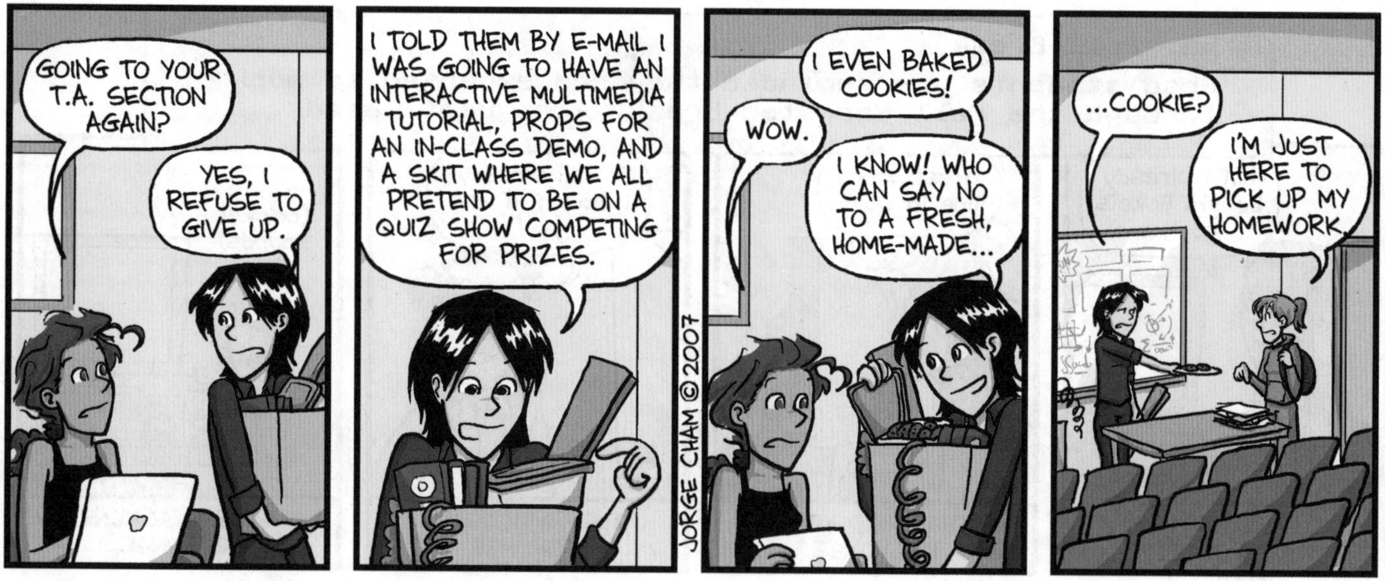

GOING TO YOUR T.A. SECTION AGAIN?
YES, I REFUSE TO GIVE UP.
I TOLD THEM BY E-MAIL I WAS GOING TO HAVE AN INTERACTIVE MULTIMEDIA TUTORIAL, PROPS FOR AN IN-CLASS DEMO, AND A SKIT WHERE WE ALL PRETEND TO BE ON A QUIZ SHOW COMPETING FOR PRIZES.
JORGE CHAM © 2007
I EVEN BAKED COOKIES!
WOW.
I KNOW! WHO CAN SAY NO TO A FRESH, HOME-MADE...
...COOKIE?
I'M JUST HERE TO PICK UP MY HOMEWORK.

THAT'S IT. I GIVE UP!
NOBODY COMES TO MY T.A. RECITATION! I DON'T GET IT!
WHEN I WAS AN UNDERGRAD, I NEVER SKIPPED CLASS! I ASKED TONS OF QUESTIONS!
JORGE CHAM © 2007
OOH!
OOH!
OK, SO I WAS KIND OF A DORK BACK THEN.
BACK THEN?
OK, LET'S SEE HOW MANY PEOPLE BOTHERED TO SHOW UP TO-
-DAY?
JORGE CHAM © 2007
WHAT HAPPENED??
YOU STOPPED MAKING HANDOUTS SO NOW WE HAVE TO PAY ATTENTION AND STUFF.
YOU MEAN THE LESS I TRY, THE MORE YOU CARE?
WE PREFER THE TERM "GRADE CONSCIOUS."

An Introduction to

QUANTUM Gradnamics

During the first half of the 20th Century, scientists struggled to explain graduation phenomena that could not be accounted for by classical Newtonian graduation mechanics*.

In particular, scientists struggled with the paradoxical *dual nature* of the relationship between grad students and their advisors.

On the one hand, graduate students were known to produce discrete papers like their supervisors and assumed to be intellectually on par with them.

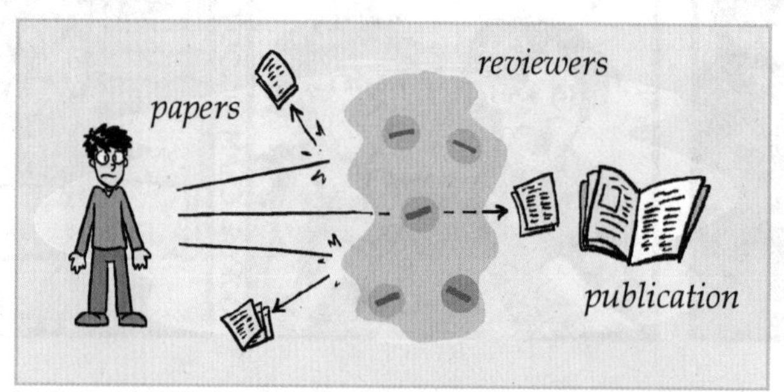

Ernest Rutherford's "Foiled Submission" experiment demonstrated that academia is made up of indiscrete matter that is largely empty.

Yet simple experiments showed that graduate students had no idea what they were doing and only followed what their supervisors told them to do.

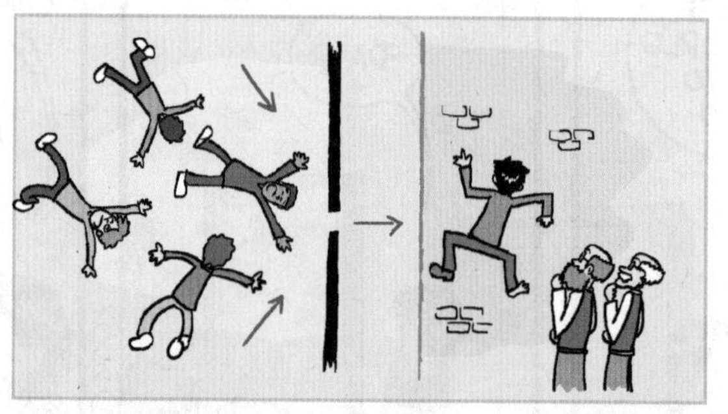

The infamous slit experiment, wherein grad students made to pass through a narrow slit (quals) are later found in a scattered and incoherent state.

Thus the question became: are graduate student indentured servants (slaves) to their supervisors, or are they as intellectually capable as professors (part equals)?

This became known as the "Slave/Part-equal Duality" and it forms the basis for the branch of physics called Quantum Gradnamics.

*see http://www.phdcomics.com/comics.php?n=221

An Introduction to

QUANTUM Gradnamics

"I discard all hope of predicting hitherto unpredictable quantities, such as my graduation."
- Werner Heisenberg

Another principal concept in Quantum Gradnamics is the observation that graduate students do not move toward graduation in a steady and continuous manner. Rather, they make progress through discrete bursts of random productivity called "wanta" (short for "want data") whose energy is proportional to the frequency of meetings with their advisor.

Grad students, or "p-ons" as Einstein called them, can only occupy a discrete number of energy states:

A direct consequence of this is the "Heisenberg Uncertain-Thesis Principle", perhaps the most well-known theorem of Quantum Gradnamics. Developed by Heisenberg during a particularly unproductive period in his graduate career, the principle states that it is not possible to know where a grad student is and where it is going at the same time:

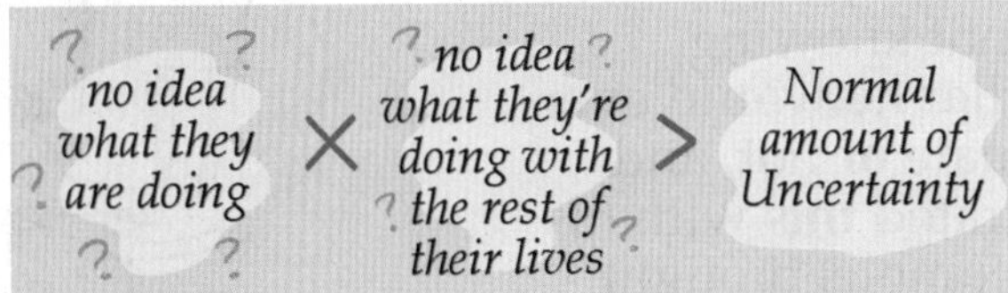

When probed under pressure, a grad student will either blurt out what they are doing (but won't know if it means anything), or they will blurt out what they *plan* to do (but won't know *how* to do it). Simply put, there is an inherent degree of certainty and precision that is missing from their everyday life.

Heisenberg attributed this to the fact that meetings with professors are *non-communicative* (that is, the order in which orders are given doesn't tell you whether they are worth doing).

An Introduction to

QUANTUM *Gradnamics*

"I had two wives at the same time. How's that for pressure to graduate!"
- Erwin Schrödinger

Although Quantum Gradnamics explains many of the phenomena in pursuing a Ph.D., most aspiring scientists still object to such an uncertain and probabilistic description of academic reality.

The Austrian scientist Erwin Schrödinger was particularly uncomfortable not knowing whether he would ever graduate or not, and illustrated this with his now famous thought experiment known as "Schrödinger's Cubicle."

1. Place grad student inside closed cubicle
2. Set up computer, coffee and internet connection
3. Wait a few years
Years

According to the experiment, grad students exist in a state of both productivity and unproductivity (many students do report feeling like...

...they're in limbo the whole time). Only direct intervention reveals whether or not an enormous amount of time has been wasted, a phenomenon known as "expectation collapse".

Einstein was also uncomfortable with this indeterminate view of academia and openly disagreed with the Copenhagen Interpretation, which states that graduation is an entirely random process. In deciding whether or not to graduate a student, Einstein famously said, "Professors don't throw dice (do they?)."

More recent theories describe grad students as soggy strings of ramen noodles, which is just as useful.

(thanks to Wikipedia for all the background info)

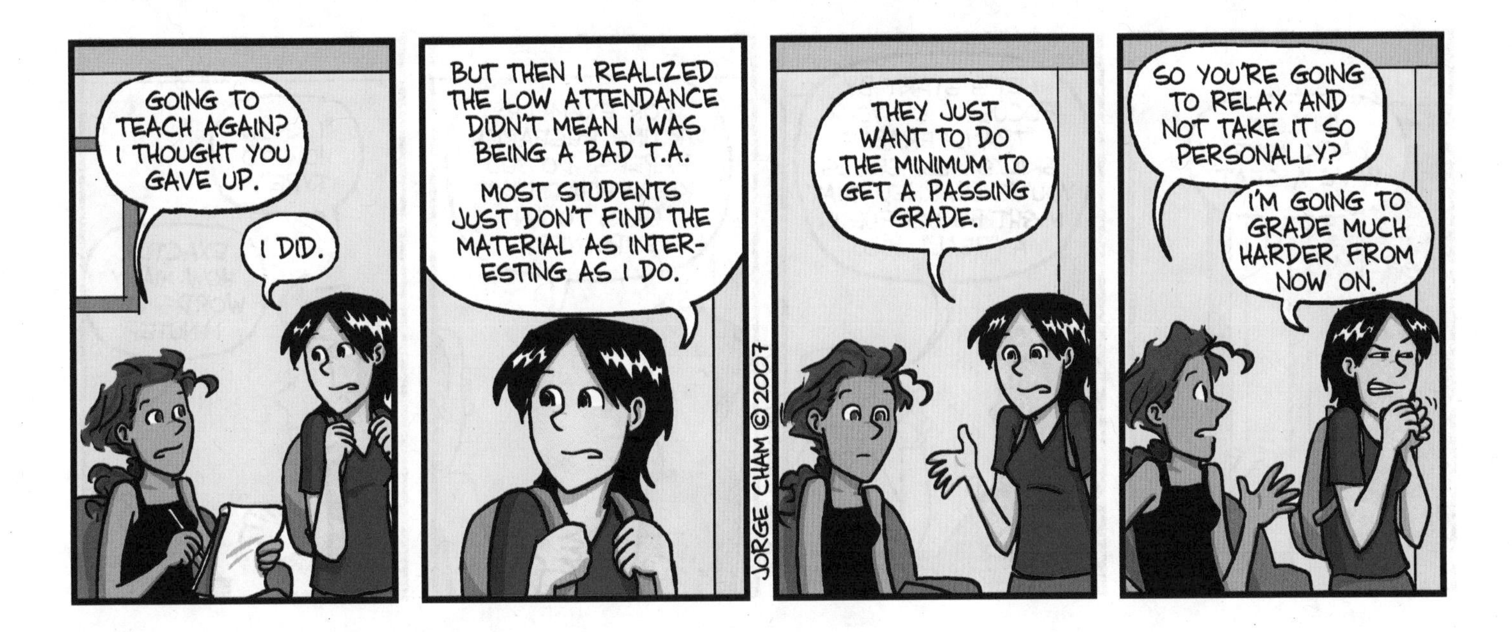

HOMECOMING! Who's excited?

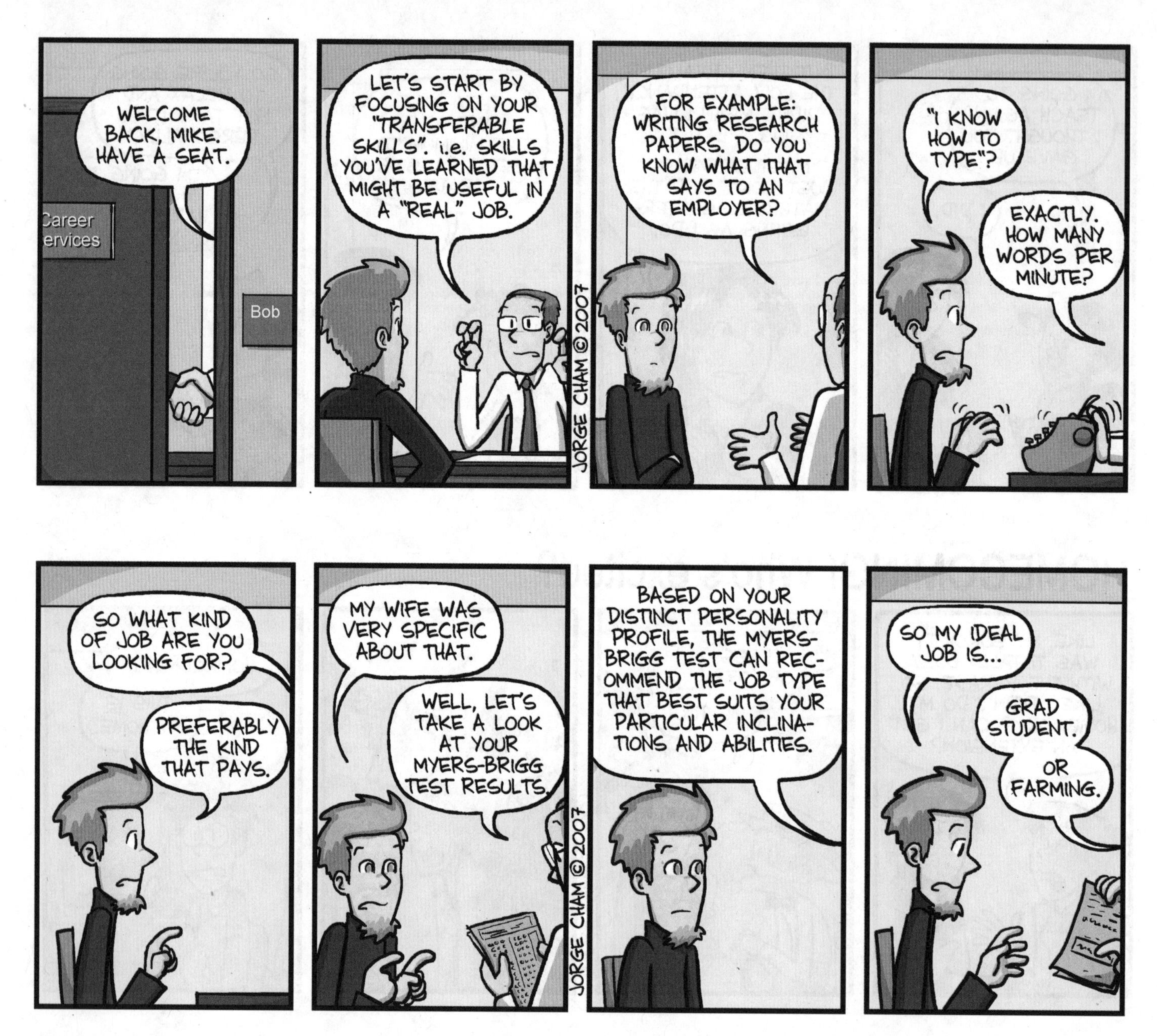
Career Services
Bob
WELCOME BACK, MIKE. HAVE A SEAT.
LET'S START BY FOCUSING ON YOUR "TRANSFERABLE SKILLS". i.e. SKILLS YOU'VE LEARNED THAT MIGHT BE USEFUL IN A "REAL" JOB.
JORGE CHAM © 2007
FOR EXAMPLE: WRITING RESEARCH PAPERS. DO YOU KNOW WHAT THAT SAYS TO AN EMPLOYER?
"I KNOW HOW TO TYPE"?
EXACTLY. HOW MANY WORDS PER MINUTE?
SO WHAT KIND OF JOB ARE YOU LOOKING FOR?
PREFERABLY THE KIND THAT PAYS.
MY WIFE WAS VERY SPECIFIC ABOUT THAT.
WELL, LET'S TAKE A LOOK AT YOUR MYERS-BRIGG TEST RESULTS.
JORGE CHAM © 2007
BASED ON YOUR DISTINCT PERSONALITY PROFILE, THE MYERS-BRIGG TEST CAN RECOMMEND THE JOB TYPE THAT BEST SUITS YOUR PARTICULAR INCLINATIONS AND ABILITIES.
SO MY IDEAL JOB IS...
GRAD STUDENT.
OR FARMING.

DID YOU TAKE A LOOK AT THOSE SLIDES I SENT?
UH-HUH, SURE.
JORGE CHAM © 2007
SIGN #137 OF A DYSFUNCTIONAL STUDENT-FACULTY RELATIONSHIP:
HAVE YOU LOOKED AT THE SECOND ORDER CORRELATIONS?
ALSO, YOUR HYPOTHESIS IS A COMPLETE JOKE.
YOUR ADVISOR ASKS MORE QUESTIONS THAN ANYBODY ELSE AT YOUR OWN SEMINAR.
ding! New Mail! from: clueless undergrad
how do i do problem 4? I'm confused!
Reply to: clueless undergrad
Ok, let's start from the beginning. Given a carrier modulated signal of the form:x(t)=a(t)cos (wct+O(t)) where a(t)= sqroot(x_I^2(t)+x_Q^2)Tan^(-1)(O), let's assume that the...
type type
JORGE CHAM © 2007
30 MINUTES LATER:
integrate over the range and take the Hilbert transform equivalent to [1+sgn(w)]X(w) for Phi positive frequen-
ding! New Mail!
type ty-
uh, never mind. i got it. lol ;) - clueless undergrad
URRGH!!
erase!

HEY HONEY, HOW'S IT GOING?
NOT BAD, ACTUALLY.
I'M EXPLORING MY OPTIONS, FOLLOWING UP ON LEADS...
JORGE CHAM © 2007
IF I PLAY MY CARDS RIGHT, I SHOULD HAVE EVERYTHING LINED UP PRETTY SOON.
I'M TALKING ABOUT YOUR JOB SEARCH, NOT "SOLITAIRE."
MY SKILLS AT THIS ARE PROBABLY IN HIGHER DEMAND THAN MY PH.D.
DON'T WORRY, FINDING A JOB IS ALL ABOUT NETWORKING.
WHO YOU KNOW, WHO THEY KNOW, WHO KNOWS THEM, WHO KNOWS THAT THEY KNOW THAT YOU KNOW THEM...
JORGE CHAM © 2007
RIGHT NOW, I HAVE MY ENTIRE NETWORK OF CONTACTS WORKING OVERTIME TO GET ME EMPLOYED.
WELL, MY COUSIN HAS A HARDWARE STORE IN MEXICO.
DOES HE NEED A PH.D.?
THEY DO NEED A MANURE SALESMAN...

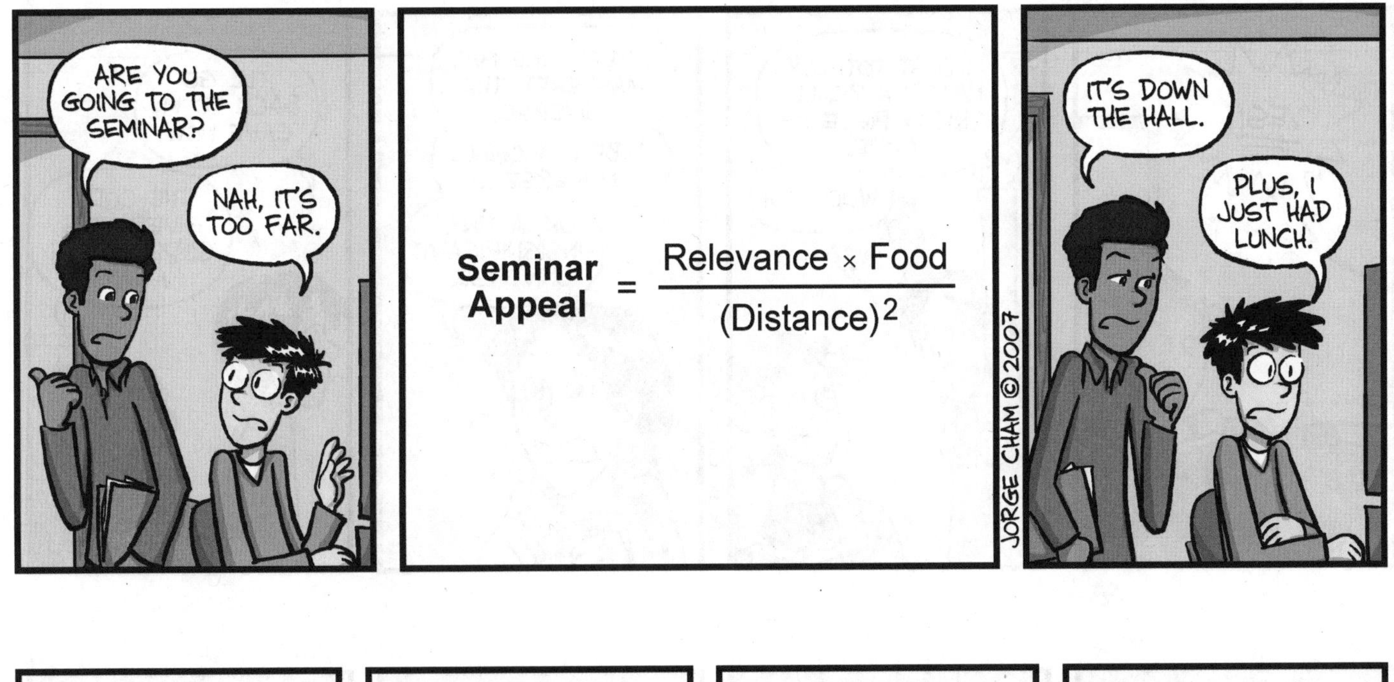
ARE YOU GOING TO THE SEMINAR?
NAH, IT'S TOO FAR.
Seminar Appeal = Relevance × Food / (Distance)²
JORGE CHAM © 2007
IT'S DOWN THE HALL.
PLUS, I JUST HAD LUNCH.

New mail!
To: All University Employees
Re: Annual Asbestos Notice
In accordance with State Health and Safety laws, we are required to remind everyone of the presence of asbestos and other harmful materials in the pipes and walls of all work buildings.
JORGE CHAM © 2007
Hopefully, these materials will not be disrupted and released into the air or leaked slowly into your drinking water.
If you breathe or smell asbestos, please notify a University official immediately.
Have a Happy Thanksgiving!
!

YES!!
I JUST TOTALLY NAILED A REALLY TRICKY PIECE OF CODE.
WOO HOO!
JORGE CHAM © 2007
I FEEL LIKE I'VE MASTERED THE UNIVERSE.
ALBEIT, A SMALL UNIVERSE...
OK, A TINY... INSIGNIFICANT UNIVERSE...
I'LL GO BACK TO MY CAVE NOW.
THE CODE GIVETH, THE CODE TAKETH AWAY.
ARE YOU GOING HOME FOR THE HOLIDAYS?
NAH, NOT THIS YEAR.
I'M A LITTLE BEHIND ON STUFF, SO I DECIDED TO STAY AND GET SOME WORK DONE.
JORGE CHAM © 2007
MY FAMILY WAS A LITTLE DISAP-POINTED, BUT I TOLD THEM MY THESIS COMES FIRST.
TICKETS WERE TOO EXPENSIVE?
EATING AND PAYING RENT ARE PRETTY IMPORTANT TOO.

Your Research Interests:

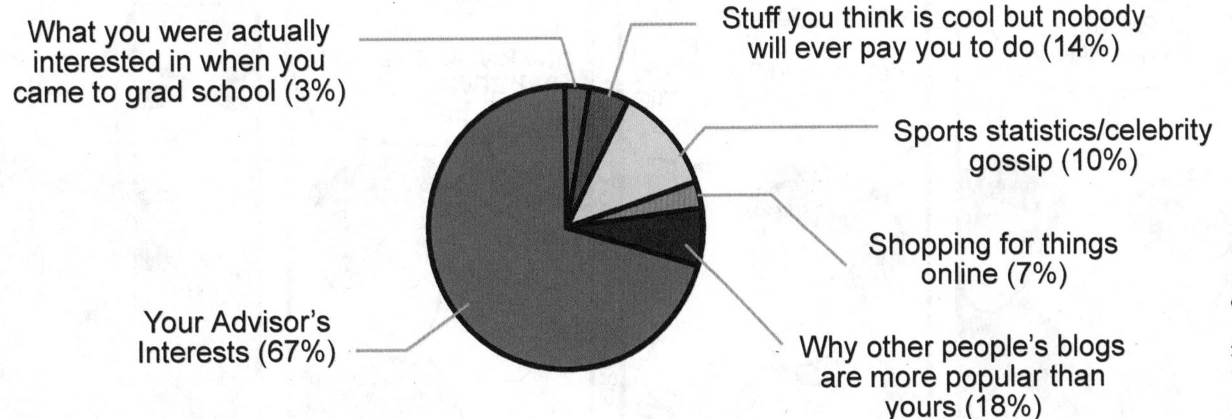

CHECK IT OUT, I GOT A SECOND MONITOR FOR MY COMPUTER.

NOW I CAN HAVE MY RESEARCH, E-MAIL, WEB-BROWSER, CHAT WINDOW AND NEWS FEEDS ALL OPEN AT THE SAME TIME!

JORGE CHAM © 2007

GETTING DISTRACTED IS SO MUCH EASIER NOW. MY PRODUCTIVITY HAS DOUBLED!

IS IT BECAUSE ZERO TIMES TWO IS STILL ZERO?

I NEED A THIRD MONITOR.

SO WHEN DO YOU WANT TO HEAD DOWN TO THE DEPARTMENT HOLIDAY PARTY?
THE SAME RULES AS HAPPY HOURS APPLY.
IF YOU GO TOO EARLY, THE PROFESSORS WILL THINK YOU'RE NOT WORKING HARD. IF YOU GO TOO LATE, ALL THE FOOD WILL BE GONE.
JORGE CHAM © 2007
BOTH THE HARDEST WORKING AND THE LAZIEST STUDENT IN THE GROUP HAVE TO WALK IN TOGETHER, OTHERWISE EVERYONE IN BETWEEN LOOKS BAD.
WAIT FOR IT... WAIT FOR IT...

SCHMOOZING WITH YOUR PROFESSOR:
JORGE CHAM © 2007
H-HEY DR. SMITH.
I'M GOING TO THE LAB AFTER THIS.
GOOD.

The DO's AND DON'Ts of SCHMOOZING WITH YOUR PROFESSOR

UH, HI.
HELLO.
I'M ONE OF PROF. SMITH'S STUDENTS.
OH, YES, BRIAN TALKS ABOUT YOU ALL THE TIME.
HE DOES??
JORGE CHAM © 2007
NO, NOT REALLY. HE'S TERRIBLE AT KEEPING TRACK OF STUDENTS.
OH. UH, HA HA.
SHE'S NOT A ROBOT!
UH, I CAN HEAR YOU.
YES, BEING MARRIED TO A PROFESSOR IS DEFINITELY...
I'VE SUFFERED ENOUGH HOLIDAY CHEER. CAN WE GO?
...INTERESTING.
JORGE CHAM © 2007
don't let him fool you. he used to goof off all the time when he was a grad student.
THAT WAS THE BEST CHRISTMAS GIFT EVER!
CAN SHE BE OUR ADVISOR?

HAPPY!
NEW!
YEAR!
STILL IN GRAD SCHOOL!
yipee.
JORGE CHAM © 2008
SO, DID YOU GET ANY WORK DONE OVER THE HOLIDAY BREAK?
OH YEAH, WITH NO ONE TO DISTRACT ME, I WAS SUPER PRODUCTIVE.
I ARCHIVED MY E-MAIL, CLEANED MY DESKTOP, FIXED THE SQUEAK IN MY OFFICE CHAIR AND TUNED THE LAB COFFEE MACHINE FOR OPTIMAL PRODUCTION.
DID YOU GET ANY REAL WORK DONE?
TO MY SENSE OF GUILT, IT'S ALL THE SAME.
JORGE CHAM © 2008

On the 12 Days of Christmas Break
my Professor gave to Me...
JORGE CHAM © 2007
12 Gigs of Data
11 Leaps of Logic
2+3=7
5×2=7
π/2=e
10 Thesis Topics
9 Poor Old Post-Docs
8 Angry Admins
7 Sloppy Seniors
JORGE CHAM © 2007

6 Cryptic E-mails
5 Futile Tasks
4 Slide Requests
JORGE CHAM © 2007
3 French Scholars
2 Bad Reviews
...and a Deadline for Next Week!
JORGE CHAM © 2007

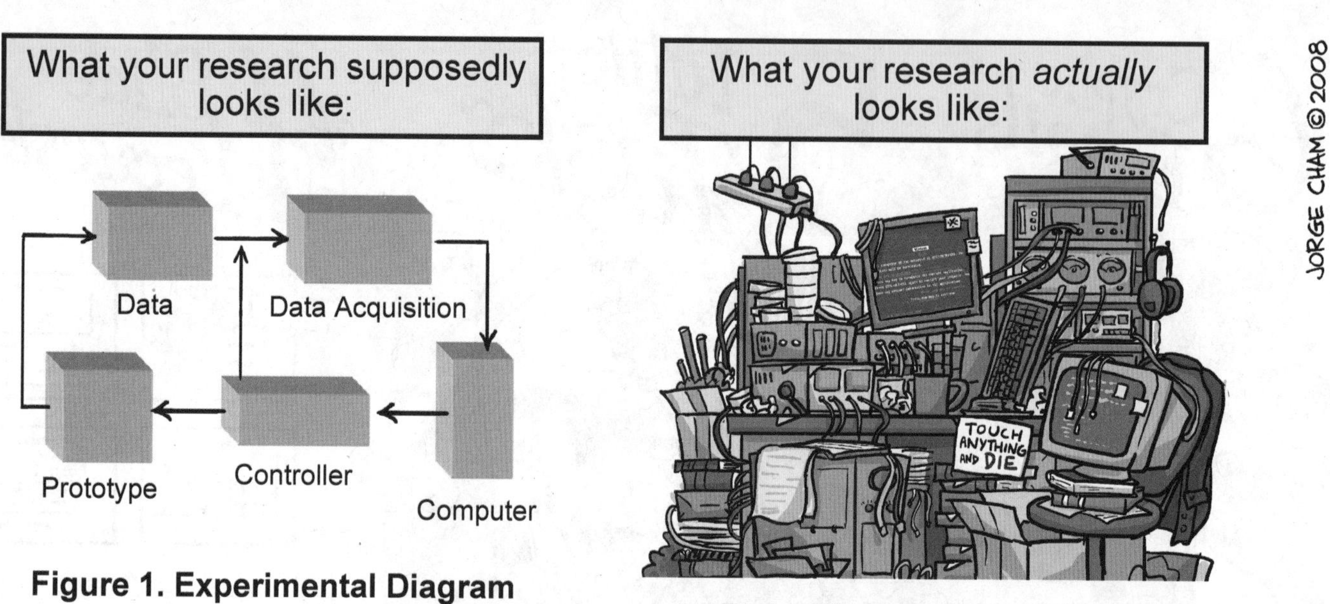
What your research supposedly looks like:
Data
Data Acquisition
Prototype
Controller
Computer
Figure 1. Experimental Diagram
What your research *actually* looks like:
TOUCH ANYTHING AND DIE
Figure 2. Experimental Mess
JORGE CHAM © 2008

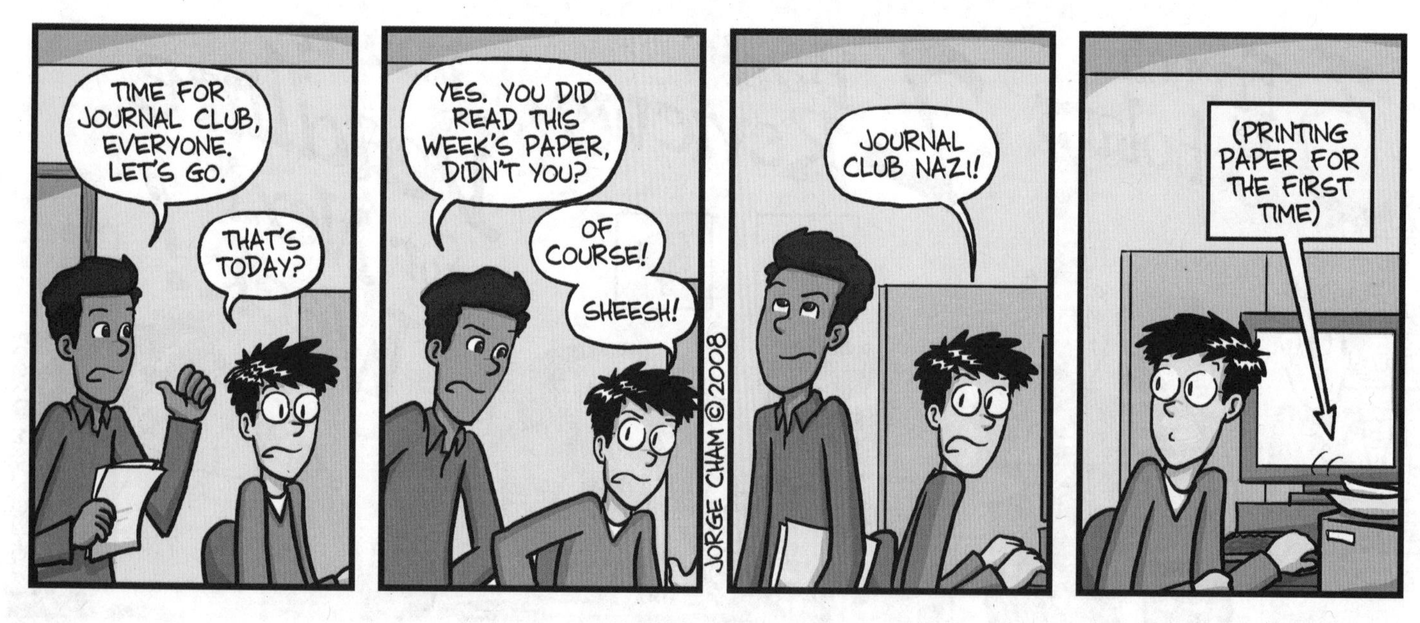
TIME FOR JOURNAL CLUB, EVERYONE. LET'S GO.
THAT'S TODAY?
YES. YOU DID READ THIS WEEK'S PAPER, DIDN'T YOU?
OF COURSE!
SHEESH!
JORGE CHAM © 2008
JOURNAL CLUB NAZI!
(PRINTING PAPER FOR THE FIRST TIME)

JOURNAL CLUB...
LET'S GO AROUND THE ROOM AND COMMENT ON THIS WEEK'S PAPER.
I THOUGHT THE MAIN HYPOTHESIS WAS WELL ARGUED BUT THE EXPERIMENTAL METHOD LACKED SOME RIGOR, ESPECIALLY THE VALIDATION SECTION.
JORGE CHAM © 2008
YES, I THOUGHT THE RESULTS COULD HAVE USED A MORE STRICT INTERPRETATION. ALSO, THE CORRELATION EQUATIONS SHOULD HAVE BEEN NORMALIZED.
THE, UH... PICTURES LOOK PRETTY.
THAT'S IT. YOU'RE FIRED.
YOU CAN'T FIRE ME FROM JOURNAL CLUB!
YES WE CAN.
THE WHOLE POINT OF DISCUSSING PAPERS ONLY MARGINALLY RELATED TO OUR THESES IS TO HONE OUR ACADEMIC SKILLS.
JORGE CHAM © 2008
IF YOU DON'T READ THE PAPER AND CONTRIBUTE, YOU'RE NOT LEARNING ANYTHING!
Paper only marginally related to your thesis
I THOUGHT THE POINT WAS TO PROCRASTINATE FROM REAL WORK.
THAT TOO. BUT WE DON'T DISCUSS THAT.

ding! new spam!
The Diploma Mill!
Get an Online PhD, only $5!
JORGE CHAM © 2007
No work necessary!
I DON'T KNOW WHETHER TO FEEL STUPID OR OUTRAGED.
LET'S CHECK IN WITH GERARD, OUR NEW HUMANITIES CHARACTER!
HOW'S IT GOING, GERARD?
GOOD! JUST DOING SOME LIGHT READING TO PREPARE FOR MY ROLE. MOSTLY ANCIENT GREEK AND SUMERIAN NARRATIVES, BUT ALSO SOME 17th CENTURY HORATIAN ODES.
JORGE CHAM © 2007
HOW IS THAT USEFUL?
USEFUL? WHAT'S THAT?
UH, SO WHEN CAN WE EXPECT JOKES FROM YOU?
5-6 YEARS? I HAVEN'T EVEN TOUCHED POST 1920 AVANT GARDE LIMMER-ICKS!

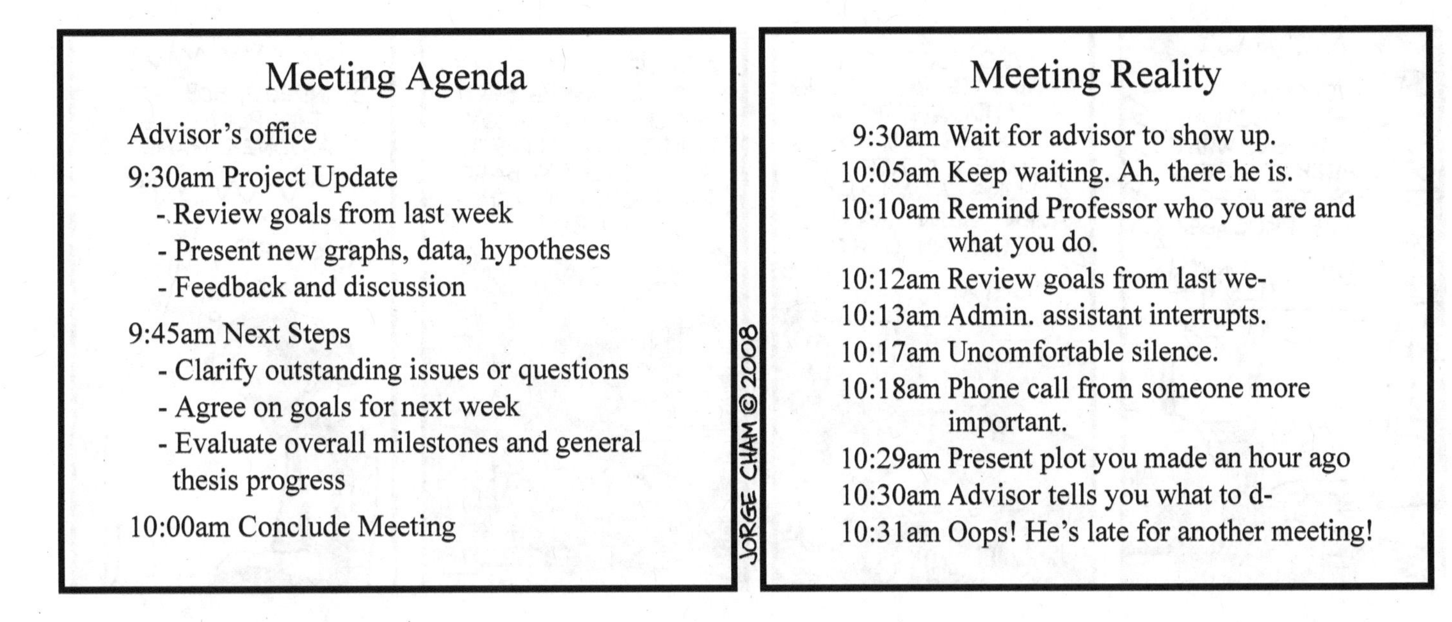
Meeting Agenda
Advisor's office
9:30am Project Update
- Review goals from last week
- Present new graphs, data, hypotheses
- Feedback and discussion
9:45am Next Steps
- Clarify outstanding issues or questions
- Agree on goals for next week
- Evaluate overall milestones and general thesis progress
10:00am Conclude Meeting
JORGE CHAM © 2008
Meeting Reality
9:30am Wait for advisor to show up.
10:05am Keep waiting. Ah, there he is.
10:10am Remind Professor who you are and what you do.
10:12am Review goals from last we-
10:13am Admin. assistant interrupts.
10:17am Uncomfortable silence.
10:18am Phone call from someone more important.
10:29am Present plot you made an hour ago
10:30am Advisor tells you what to d-
10:31am Oops! He's late for another meeting!

AHH! IT'S 5:00PM AND I HAVEN'T DONE ANYTHING TODAY!
WHY!? WHY DID I WASTE THE WHOLE DAY DOING STUPID THINGS THAT DON'T MATTER!??
JORGE CHAM © 2007
MUST... DO... SOMETHING... ANYTHING...
reads one paragraph of paper
PHEW...!
ANOTHER DAY IN GRAD SCHOOL.

WELCOME TO ESPN ELECTION COVERAGE. WHAT A WEEK IT'S BEEN FOR THE ELECTORAL PROCESS!
YES, JOHN, WITH CANDIDATE "A" CALLING CANDIDATE "B" A DOOFUS, AND "B" ISSUING A STATEMENT CALLING "A" A WUSS, I HAVENT SEEN THIS MUCH ACTION SINCE '67!!
JORGE CHAM © 2007
AND LET'S NOT COUNT OUT "C", WHO'S BEEN RACKING UP MAJOR POINTS APPEALING TO A SUBGROUP'S BASE PARANOIA AND XENOPHOBIA!
INDEED, BOB. AT THIS POINT, IT'S ANYONE'S GAME!
"GAME"?
AHH...
THERE'S NOTHING LIKE SPENDING A QUIET EVENING AT HOME...
JORGE CHAM © 2008
JUST ME, SOME CHOCOLATES...
...AND 200 PAPERS TO GRADE.

GRADING: THE FIRST HOUR.
good job!
nice!
oops!
Well Done!
SECOND HOUR
HOW CAN YOU GET THIS WRONG?? I COVERED IT LIKE FIFTY TIMES!!
JORGE CHAM © 2008
SIXTH HOUR
I DON'T CARE ANYMORE! WHEN WILL IT END???
HOUR 20
IF UNDERGRADS ARE THE FUTURE, WE'RE **ALL DOOMED**.
WHOA. WHAT ARE YOU DOING, CECILIA?
JORGE CHAM © 2008
CRUSHING THE DREAMS OF OUR YOUTH. YOU?
YOU'RE STAPLING TACO BELL APPLICATIONS TO THEIR PAPERS??

OK, CHECK OUT WHAT THIS UNDERGRAD WROTE...
"GIVEN A SIGNAL WITH A 2-Hz BANDWAGON, THE NYQUIL FREQUENCY MUST BE 1-Hz TO AVOID ALIENING OF THE FURRIER TRANSFORMER."
JORGE CHAM © 2008
I TAKE IT THAT'S WRONG?
WRONG? IT'S DOWNRIGHT PATHETIC!
1-Hz!? come on!
CECILIA, I KNOW GRADING UNDERGRAD PAPERS CAN BE DISCOURAGING, BUT YOU HAVE TO REALIZE...
...THEY'RE NOT ALL GOING TO GET A PH.D.
JORGE CHAM © 2008
MOST UNDERGRADS ARE JUST GOING TO TRADITIONAL JOBS LIKE BEING A DOCTOR, A PILOT, GRADE SCHOOL TEACHER... LAW MAKER...
IS THAT SUPPOSED TO MAKE ME FEEL BETTER?
ABOUT FAILING THEM, YES.

WOW. THERE ISN'T A SINGLE MISTAKE ON THIS PAPER.
SOMEBODY ACTUALLY GOT IT RIGHT!
FINALLY! I CAN'T BELIE-
JORGE CHAM © 2008
THIS IS THE ANSWER KEY.
I MADE THIS.
DONE!! FINALLY!!
JORGE CHAM © 2008
IN
OUT

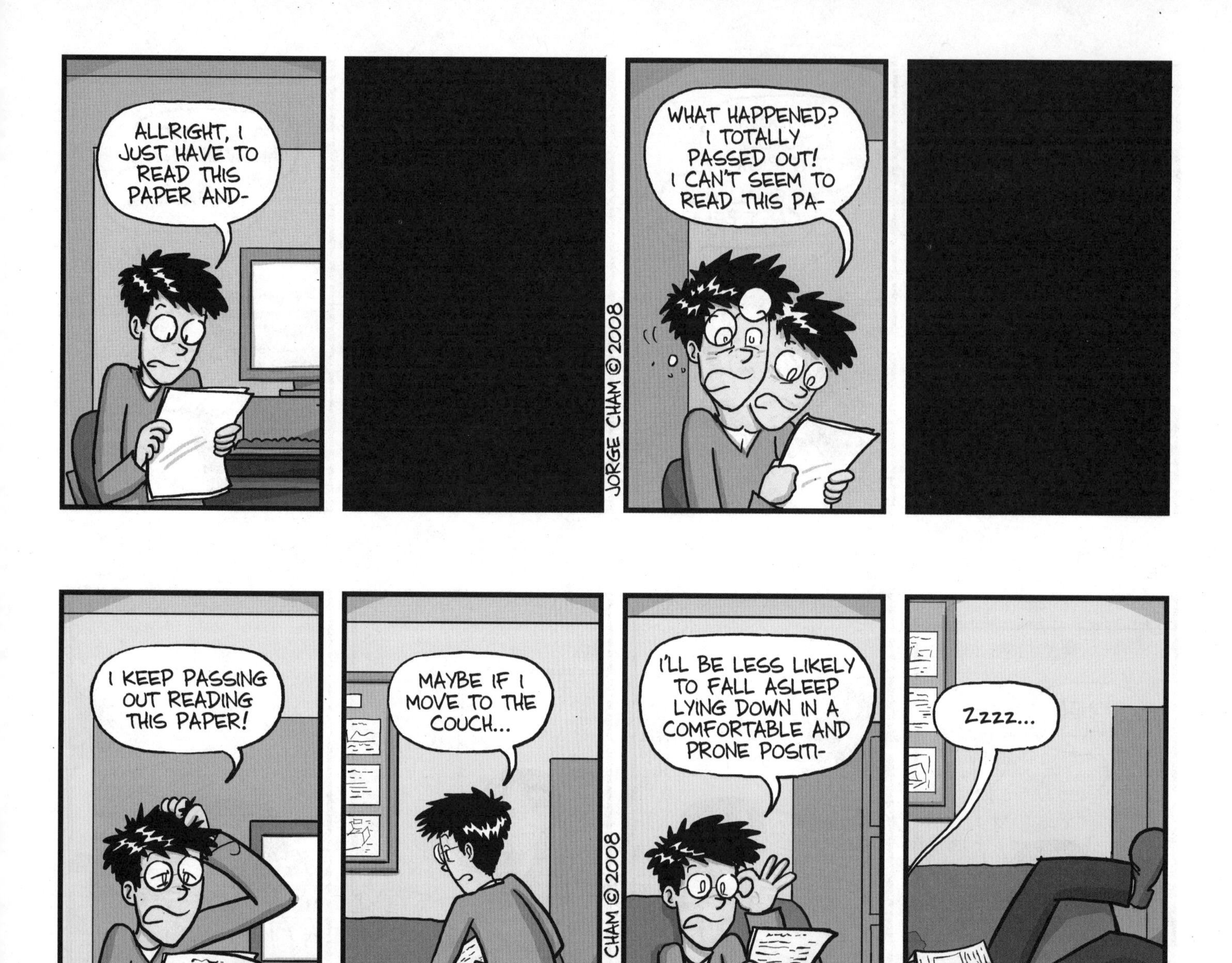
ALLRIGHT, I JUST HAVE TO READ THIS PAPER AND-
JORGE CHAM © 2008
WHAT HAPPENED? I TOTALLY PASSED OUT! I CAN'T SEEM TO READ THIS PA-
I KEEP PASSING OUT READING THIS PAPER!
MAYBE IF I MOVE TO THE COUCH...
JORGE CHAM © 2008
I'LL BE LESS LIKELY TO FALL ASLEEP LYING DOWN IN A COMFORTABLE AND PRONE POSITI-
Zzzz...
THE SAD LOGIC OF DESPERATE GRAD STUDENTS.

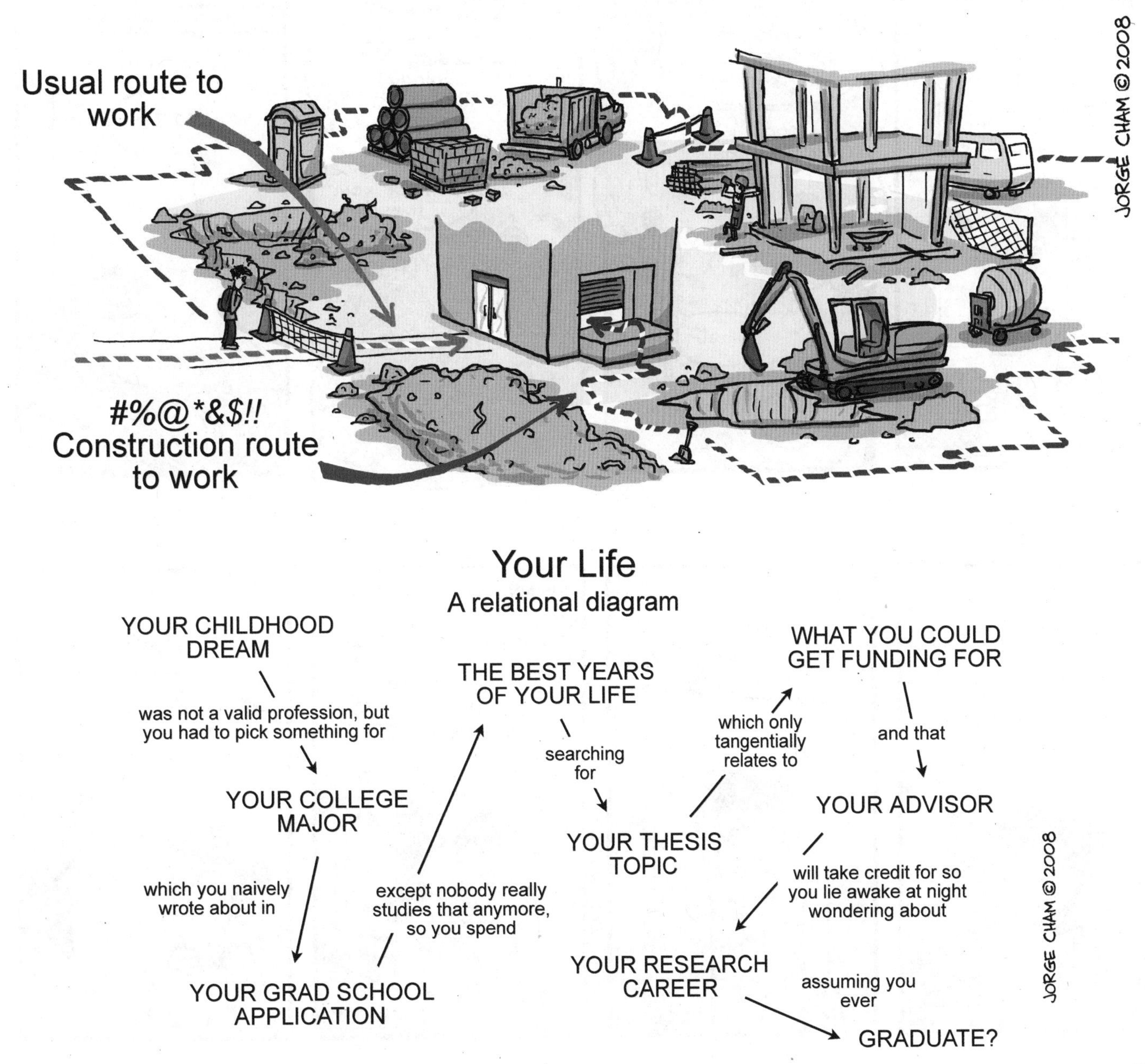
Usual route to work
#%@*&$!! Construction route to work
JORGE CHAM © 2008
Your Life
A relational diagram
YOUR CHILDHOOD DREAM
was not a valid profession, but you had to pick something for
YOUR COLLEGE MAJOR
which you naively wrote about in
YOUR GRAD SCHOOL APPLICATION
except nobody really studies that anymore, so you spend
THE BEST YEARS OF YOUR LIFE
searching for
YOUR THESIS TOPIC
which only tangentially relates to
WHAT YOU COULD GET FUNDING FOR
and that
YOUR ADVISOR
will take credit for so you lie awake at night wondering about
YOUR RESEARCH CAREER
assuming you ever
GRADUATE?
JORGE CHAM © 2008

C-C...
COFFEE...
Adenosine receptors have been blocked, sir!
good. let's hope that-
CAFFEINE
CH_3
what?
he's reading the methodology section!
it's all in the passive voice! run for your lives!!
Therefore
JORGE CHAM © 2008
ZZZ...
A-ACKNOWLEDGEMENTS AND...
THERE! I FINISHED READING THIS PAPER!
AND IT ONLY TOOK...
JORGE CHAM © 2008
...ALL DAY!??
IT TOOK ME ALL DAY TO READ ONE PAPER??
SO WHAT'S IT ABOUT?
I WAS SUPPOSED TO PAY ATTENTION?

IT'S 3am AND MOST OF YOUR FRIENDS ARE SAFE AND ASLEEP.
BUT THERE'S A PHONE IN THE LAB AND IT'S RINGING...
SOMETHING NEEDS TO BE HAPPENING IN TERMS OF RESEARCH.
JORGE CHAM © 2008
WHO DO YOU THINK SHOULD BE THERE TO ANSWER THAT PHONE?
YOU, OF COURSE.
MY NAME IS PROF. SMITH AND I APPROVE THIS MESSAGE.

SO, DID YOU DO WHAT I TOLD YOU TO DO LAST WEEK?
UH...
I'M SORRY, PROF. SMITH, I TRIED BUT I COULDN'T GET IT TO WORK!
HMMM...
JORGE CHAM © 2008
PERHAPS I WAS TOO AMBITIOUS IN SETTING THE GOALS FOR THIS PROJECT...
OR PERHAPS YOU'RE NOT SMART ENOUGH TO CARRY OUT THE GRANDEUR OF MY VISION.
GUESS WHICH ONE I THINK IT IS.
not the first?

HONEY, MAYBE IT WOULD HELP YOUR JOB SEARCH IF YOU THOUGHT ABOUT YOUR LIFE GOALS.
I MEAN, WHAT SORT OF CAREER DID YOU HAVE IN MIND WHEN YOU WENT TO GRAD SCHOOL?
JORGE CHAM © 2008
WHAT DID YOU ENVISION DOING WITH YOUR PH.D.?
WHAT DO YOU WANT TO BE WHEN YOU GROW UP?
RETIRED.
HELLO?
GOOD NEWS, MIKE. I GOT YOU AN INTERVIEW.
JORGE CHAM © 2008
UH, WHAT'S THAT, BOB?
DO I OWN A "SUIT"?
these are tears of joy!

WHAT KIND OF GROWN MAN DOESN'T OWN A SUIT?
WHAT ABOUT MY WEDDING SUIT?
JORGE CHAM © 2008
WE ELOPED IN LAS VEGAS, REMEMBER?
YOU WORE SHORTS.
IT'S A LITTLE BIG.
IT'S ON SALE.
WE'LL TAKE IT.
MIKE INTERVIEWS FOR A JOB:
COME IN, MIKE. HAVE A SEAT.
I HAVE TO SAY, WE ARE VERY IMPRESSED WITH YOUR RESUME.
RIGHT ON.
ALTHOUGH...
JORGE CHAM © 2008
...I THINK YOU MADE A TYPO.
IT SAYS HERE YOU STARTED GRAD SCHOOL IN THE 1980'S.
UH...
YEAH, THAT'S A MISTAKE.
THE TYPO OR STARTING GRAD SCHOOL?

OK, MIKE, HERE IS A PUZZLE WE GIVE TO ALL OUR INTERVIEWEES...
SUPPOSE N NUMBER OF PEOPLE HAVE X COINS, BUT NONE OF THEM HAVE POCKETS, HOW MANY EGGS MUST THEY BREAK TO CROSS THE RIVER ASSUMING THE FOX WILL EAT THE CHICKEN?
JORGE CHAM © 2008
UH...
FOUR?
WOW, THAT'S RIGHT!
HOW DID YOU DO IT??
I READ IT ON THE INTERNET.
THAT'S PH.D. TRAINING.
MIKE, WE WANT TO MAKE YOU A JOB OFFER.
SHARP ANALYTICAL SKILLS IS ONE OF THE REASONS WE LIKE TO HIRE PH.D.'S
SO, NAME YOUR PRICE.
JORGE CHAM © 2008
WELL, IN TERMS OF SALARY, I KNOW WHAT I'M WORTH AND I WILL NOT ACCEPT ANYTHING LESS THAN...
...WHAT I CURRENTLY MAKE AS A GRAD STUDENT.
LOW EXPECTATIONS IS THE OTHER REASON.

MIKE, THIS IS WHAT WE'RE PREPARED TO PAY YOU TO COME WORK FOR US.
THIS IS TEN TIMES WHAT I MAKE AS A GRAD STUDENT.
WELCOME TO THE REAL WORLD.
I, UH...
JORGE CHAM © 2008
I NEED TO, UM...
HEY!
HOW DID THE INTERVIEW GO??
I, UH...
I DON'T THINK IT'S GOING TO WORK OUT.
JORGE CHAM © 2008
AW, THAT'S OK, HONEY. I'M SURE SOMETHING WILL COME UP SOON.
WE HAVE FAITH IN YOU.
YOU DON'T MIND GOING TO PUBLIC SCHOOLS, DO YOU?
da!

unit tests passed!
YES!
CELEBRATORY DANCE!
JORGE CHAM © 2008
OH YEAH, WHO'S GOOD?
UH-H...
WHY IT'S NOT A GOOD IDEA TO SIT WITH YOUR BACK TO THE DOOR.
...HI, PROF. JONES.
let's skip this part of the tour.
HAVE YOU BEEN FOLLOWING THE ELECTION THIS YEAR?
NO. I WAS SO HEART-BROKEN AFTER THE LAST TWO PRESIDENTIAL ELECTIONS, I DECIDED NOT TO GET EMOTIONALLY INVOLVED THIS TIME AROUND.
JORGE CHAM © 2008
THE DEMOCRATS ARE DESTROYING THEMSELVES.
I KNEW IT!!

ARCHITECTURAL STYLES
OF CONTEMPORARY UNIVERSITIES

A guide to the richness of design that you probably ignore on your way to work as you walk with your head down absorbed in thought.

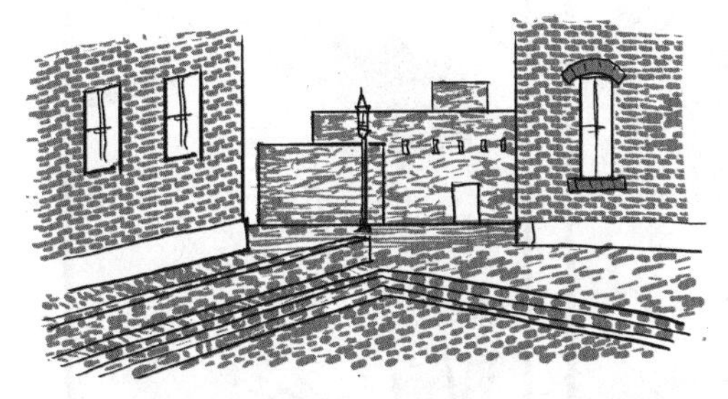

Red Brick Wonderland (c. 1800's)
There are more bricks on campus than books. Not recommended: wearing red at busy intersections.

"Gothic Envyist" (c. 1600-1700's)
Nothing says "We're just like Oxford and Cambridge!" like cheerful gothic architecture from the middle ages.

Modernist "It cost HOW much??" (1990's-present)
Sure, they could have built three buildings for the same price, but those buildings would be functional and non-leaking.

Neo-Penal (1960-1970's)
Influenced by nouveau prison design and the need to quell student riots, concrete structures of this period have the unique ability to <u>*drain your very Life Force*</u>.

The Campus Tower

No respectable institution of higher learning would be complete without a towering symbol of ence-phalic domination (also makes a good tourist photo-op).

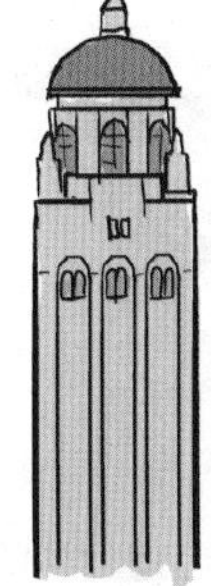

Stanford's Hoove Tower

Window details:

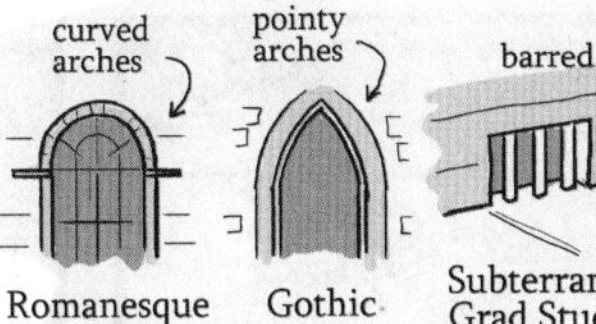

Finally...

A Designed Environment
Despite differences in styles, all academic architecture has the same purpose: to ~~create an environment that inspires and fosters learning and intellectual discourse.~~
convince alumni and parents they're getting their money's worth.

I HAVE SOME GOOD NEWS AND SOME BAD NEWS.
THE GOOD NEWS IS WE'VE BEEN INVITED TO A PRESTIGIOUS CONFERENCE AT A RESORT IN ACAPULCO.
JORGE CHAM © 2008
THE BAD NEWS IS YOU HAVE TO WRITE THE PAPER AND THE DEADLINE IS IN FIVE HOURS.
ALSO, I'M GOING TO ACAPULCO, NOT YOU.
I GUESS THE GOOD NEWS ONLY APPLIES TO ME.
HOURS UNTIL PAPER DEADLINE:
01:15:24
AAHH!
00:00:17
come on come on come on...
ding! new mail!
JORGE CHAM © 2008
Due to the over-whelming number of requests, we have extended the paper deadline one week.
- Conference Organizers
AARGHH!
168:00:00
DUDE, THEY ALWAYS EXTEND THE DEADLINE.
i have to work on this for another week??

Your Profile Picture

Perhaps the most important decision of your day.

The Goofy Close-up

Personal Info:

"OMG, like, haha ROTFL!!!!!"

You in exotic location/participating in extreme sport

Activities:

"Been there, done that."

Your baby picture (aww!)

About me:

"I *used* to be cute... WHAT HAPPENED??"

You with significant other

Relationship:

"See? I'm not the only person who likes me."

The casual snapshot

Status:

"Like, whatever, i didn't just spend 3 hours trying to pick my profile picture."

JORGE CHAM © 2008

HOW MIKE SLACKENERNY FINALLY GETS A JOB:
HAVE YOU FOUND A JOB YET?
NOPE.
JORGE CHAM © 2008
DO YOU WANT TO BE MY POSTDOC?
SURE.
(WE DIDN'T SAY IT WAS A REAL JOB)
SO, WHAT'S MY JOB AS A POSTDOC?
IT'S PRETTY MUCH THE SAME AS YOUR LAST YEAR IN GRAD SCHOOL, EXCEPT YOU DON'T HAVE TO WRITE A THESIS AND YOU GET PAID TWICE AS MUCH.
JORGE CHAM © 2008
THAT'S IT?
YES.
DO I GET TWICE THE RESPECT?
SOME. ANYTHING IS BETTER THAN NOTHING.

WAIT, SO ALL THIS TIME YOU COULD HAVE BEEN PAYING ME TWICE WHAT I WAS MAKING?
YES, GRANTS USUALLY PROVIDE FOR TWICE WHAT YOU ACTUALLY GET PAID, BUT THE UNIVERSITY KEEPS HALF OF IT FOR "TUITION".
JORGE CHAM © 2008
NOW THAT YOU'RE A "DOCTOR", WE HAVE NO EXCUSE TO KEEP THAT MONEY SO WE GIVE IT TO YOU.
GEE, THANKS.
DON'T MENTION IT.
SERIOUSLY, DON'T TELL THE GRAD STUDENTS.
A POST-DOC IS A WIN-WIN SITUATION FOR THE TWO OF US.
YOU GET TO KEEP DOING EXACTLY WHAT YOU'RE DOING NOW...
JORGE CHAM © 2008
I GET CHEAP LABOR WITHOUT HAVING TO TRAIN SOMEONE FROM SCRATCH.
WAIT, WE BOTH WIN, OR YOU WIN TWICE?
THE POINT IS, AT LEAST ONE OF US WINS.

A POST-DOC IS ALMOST A REQUIREMENT FOR AN ACADEMIC CAREER THESE DAYS.
EMPLOYERS WANT TO SEE HOW WELL YOU PERFORM AS AN INDEPENDENT RESEARCHER BEFORE THEY HIRE YOU.
JORGE CHAM © 2008
DO I REALLY HAVE THAT MUCH INDEPENDENCE?
IN THEORY, NO...
...BUT GIVEN HOW MUCH I'LL IGNORE YOU, YES.
CAN I HAVE THAT IN WRITING?

HAPPY BIRTHDAY, CECILIA!!
HEY, GUYS! THANKS FOR COMING!
AWW, CHOCOLATES..! THAT'S AWESOME, THANK YOU!
JORGE CHAM © 2008
EVERYBODY IS IN THE BACK. HELP YOURSELVES TO FOOD AND DRINK!
best. birthday. ever.

HAHA, TOTALLY!
ISN'T THAT RIGHT, CECILIA?
...CECILIA?
JORGE CHAM © 2008
ARE YOU CHECKING E-MAIL??
IT'S MY PARTY AND I'LL WORK IF I WANT TO!
CECILIA, IT'S YOUR BIRTHDAY! SHOULDN'T YOU BE HAVING FUN?
BUT I DON'T REMEMBER HOW TO HAVE F-
JORGE CHAM © 2008
WHAT HAPPENED? IS SHE DRUNK?
SHE ATE ALL THE CHOCOLATE.

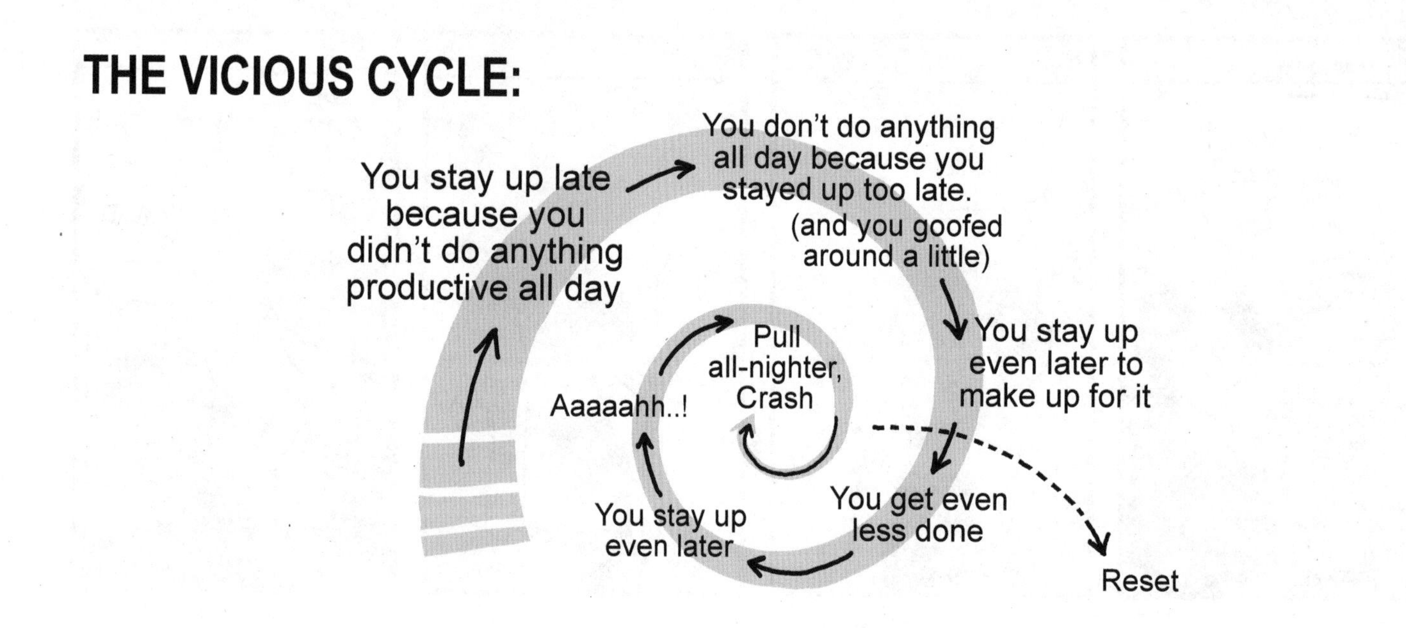
THE VICIOUS CYCLE:
You stay up late because you didn't do anything productive all day
You don't do anything all day because you stayed up too late.
(and you goofed around a little)
You stay up even later to make up for it
You get even less done
You stay up even later
Aaaaahh..!
Pull all-nighter, Crash
Reset
JORGE CHAM © 2008

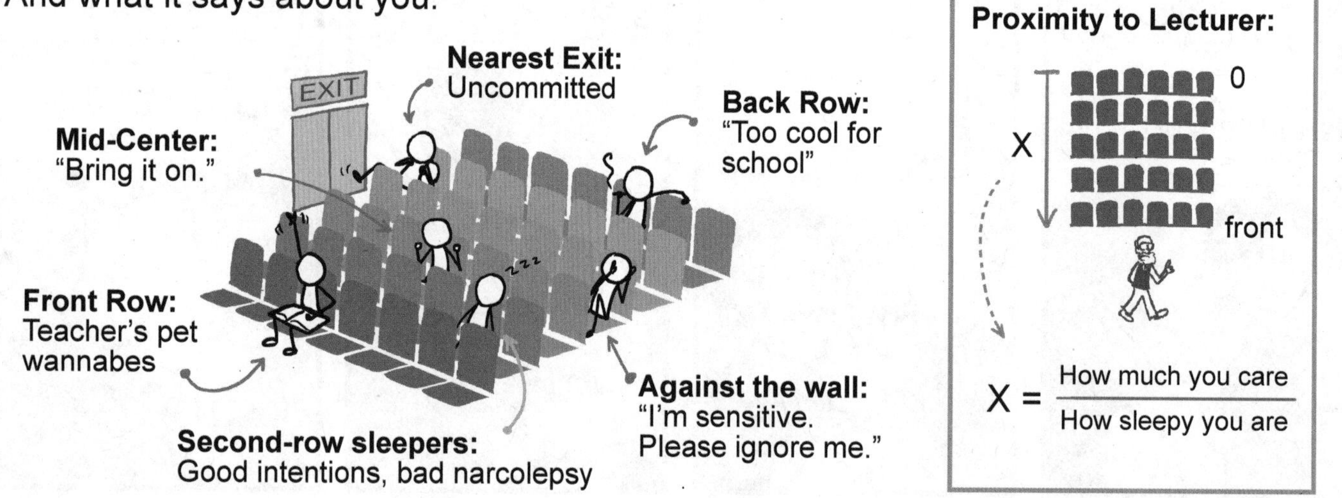
WHERE YOU SIT IN CLASS/SEMINAR
And what it says about you:
EXIT
Nearest Exit:
Uncommitted
Mid-Center:
"Bring it on."
Back Row:
"Too cool for school"
Front Row:
Teacher's pet wannabes
Second-row sleepers:
Good intentions, bad narcolepsy
Against the wall:
"I'm sensitive. Please ignore me."
Proximity to Lecturer:
0
X
front
X = How much you care / How sleepy you are
JORGE CHAM © 2008

YOUR LIFE AMBITION - What Happened??

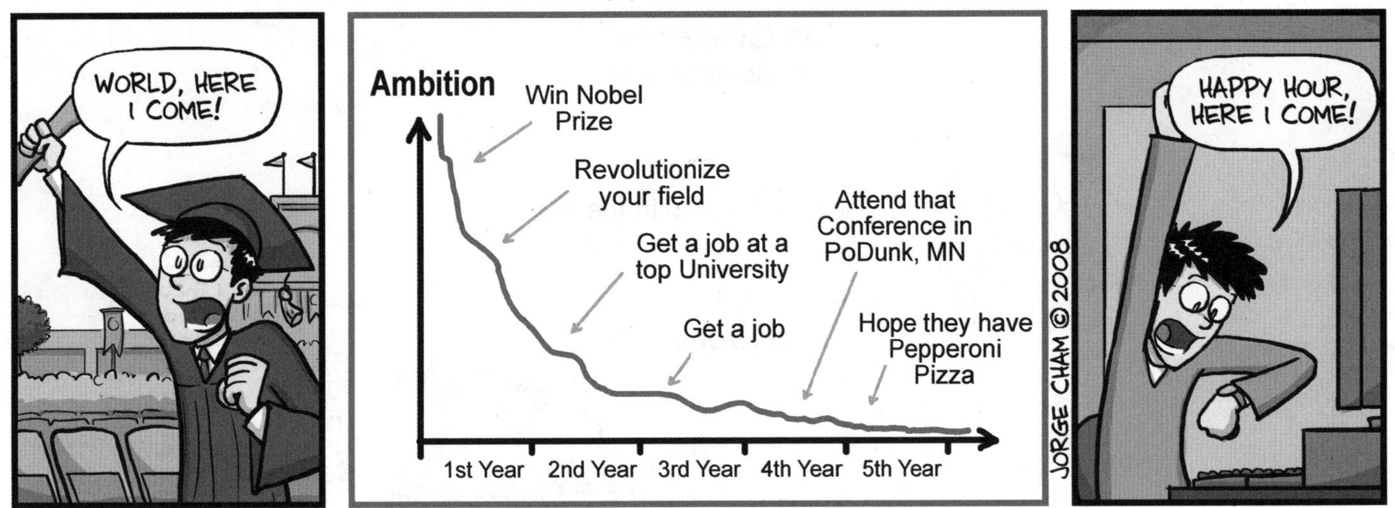

Go Green Renewable strategies for a sustainable academic career

Recycle (ideas)

This Paper made from **30%** post-published material

Reduce your On-lab Footprint.

Exit

Switch to Alternative Fuel Sources.

Eat local.

JORGE CHAM © 2008

THE LAB HIERARCHY

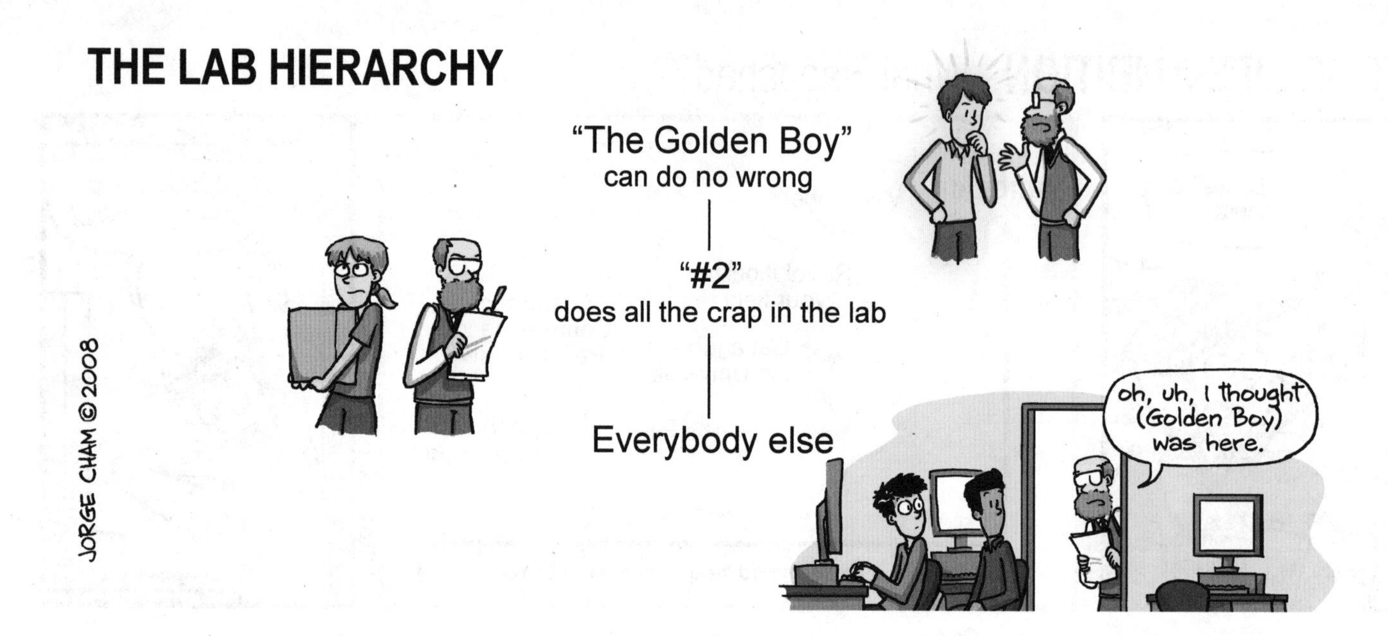

"The Golden Boy"
can do no wrong

WHEN TO MEET WITH YOUR ADVISOR Is there ever a good time?

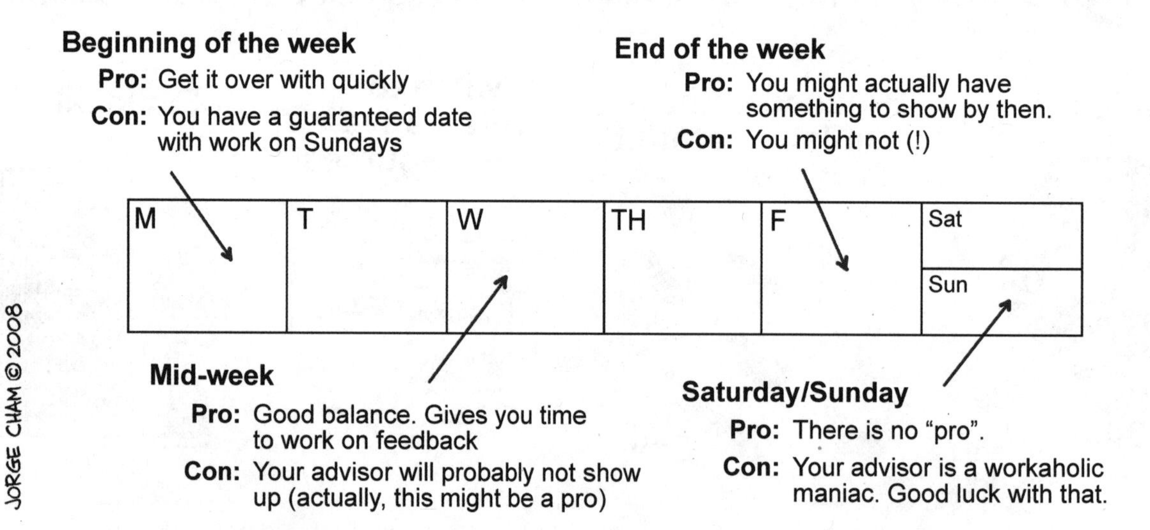

Beginning of the week
Pro: Get it over with quickly
Con: You have a guaranteed date with work on Sundays
End of the week
Pro: You might actually have something to show by then.
Con: You might not (!)
M
T
W
TH
F
Sat
Sun
Mid-week
Pro: Good balance. Gives you time to work on feedback
Con: Your advisor will probably not show up (actually, this might be a pro)
Saturday/Sunday
Pro: There is no "pro".
Con: Your advisor is a workaholic maniac. Good luck with that.
does all the crap in the lab
Everybody else
oh, uh, I thought (Golden Boy) was here.
JORGE CHAM © 2008

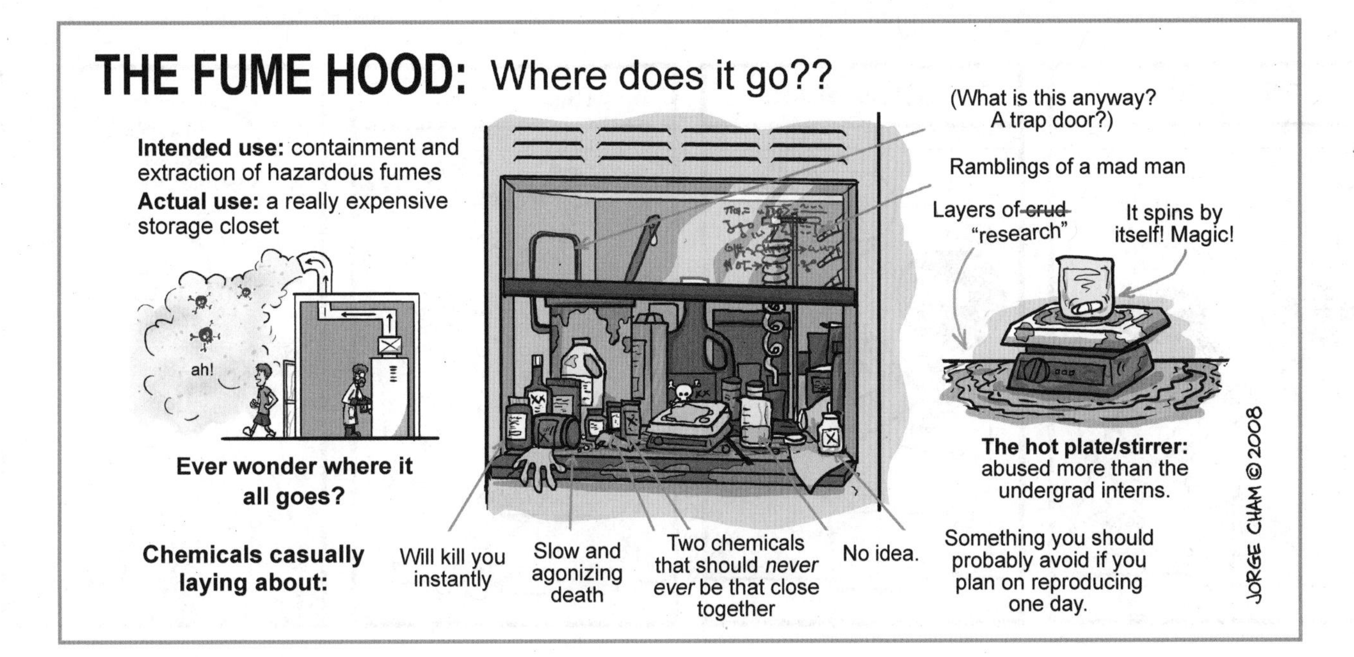
THE FUME HOOD: Where does it go??
Intended use: containment and extraction of hazardous fumes
Actual use: a really expensive storage closet
ah!
Ever wonder where it all goes?
(What is this anyway? A trap door?)
Ramblings of a mad man
Layers of crud "research"
It spins by itself! Magic!
The hot plate/stirrer: abused more than the undergrad interns.
Chemicals casually laying about:
Will kill you instantly
Slow and agonizing death
Two chemicals that should never ever be that close together
No idea.
Something you should probably avoid if you plan on reproducing one day.
JORGE CHAM © 2008

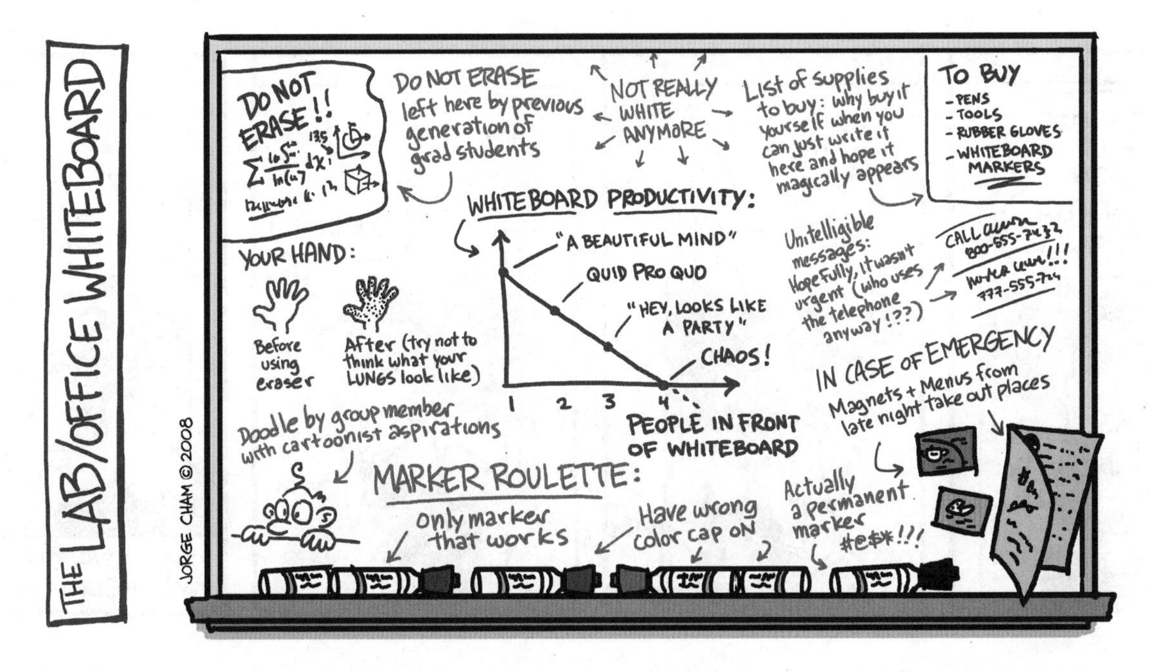
THE LAB/OFFICE WHITEBOARD
DO NOT ERASE!!
DO NOT ERASE left here by previous generation of grad students
NOT REALLY WHITE ANYMORE
List of supplies to buy: why buy it yourself when you can just write it here and hope it magically appears
TO BUY
- PENS
- TOOLS
- RUBBER GLOVES
- WHITEBOARD MARKERS
WHITEBOARD PRODUCTIVITY:
"A BEAUTIFUL MIND"
QUID PRO QUO
"HEY, LOOKS LIKE A PARTY"
CHAOS!
1 2 3 4
PEOPLE IN FRONT OF WHITEBOARD
YOUR HAND:
Before using eraser
After (try not to think what your LUNGS look like)
Unitelligible messages: Hopefully, it wasn't urgent (who uses the telephone anyway!??)
IN CASE OF EMERGENCY
Magnets + Menus from late night take out places
Doodle by group member with cartoonist aspirations
MARKER ROULETTE:
Only marker that works
Have wrong color cap ON
Actually a permanent marker #@$*!!!
JORGE CHAM © 2008

FIRST YEAR:
DOH!
SECOND YEAR:
ARGH!
JORGE CHAM © 2008
THIRD YEAR:
#&@%!!
MAYBE YOU SHOULD TRY SOMETHING ELSE.
NOW YOU TELL ME??
YES, HI, I NEED TO LOOK UP MY RECORD?
MY NAME IS TAJEL.
THAT'S T-A-J-
JORGE CHAM © 2008
NO, "J" AS IN,
UH...
JUMBO?
YES, "J"
NO, I-
I'M PRETTY SURE I KNOW HOW TO SPELL MY NAME.
THE JOYS OF HAVING AN UNCOMMON NAME.

WE HAVE A SURPLUS IN THE BUDGET THAT WE NEED TO SPEND.
IF WE DON'T SPEND IT, WE MIGHT LOSE IT OR GET LESS MONEY NEXT TIME.
JORGE CHAM © 2008
SO, IF THERE IS ANYTHING YOU NEED TO BUY, NO MATTER HOW TRIVIAL, NON-URGENT OR UNNECESSARY, NOW IS THE TIME TO GET IT.
CAN I GET A RAISE?
I SAID SPEND THE MONEY, NOT WASTE IT.
JORGE CHAM © 2008
PROXIMITY CARD ACCESS: MAYBE YOU SHOULD TAKE IT OUT OF YOUR WALLET.
C'MON!

I DON'T UNDERSTAND WHY YOU'RE NOT MAKING PROGRESS ON YOUR THESIS.
YOU NEED TO STOP GETTING DISTRACTED AND FOCUS EXCLUSIVELY ON YOUR RESEARCH.
JORGE CHAM © 2008
BY THE WAY, DID YOU FINISH THAT SIDE PROJECT I ASSIGNED YOU?
ALSO, YOU NEED TO FIX THE LAB EQUIPMENT, UPGRADE THE SERVERS AND PREPARE NEW SLIDES.
WAIT, WHICH PART DO YOU NOT UNDERSTAND?
THE PART THAT YOU'RE STILL HERE WASTING TIME. GO! GO!

TODAY IS A HOLIDAY AND I AM NOT GOING TO WORK!
I'M JUST GOING TO SIT HERE, RELAX AND...
JORGE CHAM © 2008
AND...
WHY DO I EVEN BOTHER?

I'M SUPPOSED TO ATTEND AN IMPORTANT CONFERENCE NEXT WEEK, BUT I WON'T BE ABLE TO GO.
OOH! SEND ME!
IT'S A SHAME TOO, BECAUSE IT'S A VERY PRESTIGIOUS EVENT.
PLLLEASE PLEASE SEND ME!
JORGE CHAM © 2008
EVERYONE WHO'S ANYONE IS GOING TO BE THERE.
SENDMESENDME SENDMESEND...
DO YOU WANT TO GO?
THAT WORKED??
OK.
GUESS WHO'S BEING SENT TO A PRESTIGIOUS CONFERENCE?
YOU?
YES!
IT'S IN THE SOUTH OF FRANCE!
OOH, I'M JEALOUS!
JORGE CHAM © 2008
I BETTER START PACKING!
HOLD MY PASSPORT?
FINALLY! THINGS ARE WORKING OUT FOR ME!
DID YOU KNOW YOUR STUDENT VISA IS EXPIRED?

MY VISA IS EXPIRED??
HOW CAN THAT BE!?
IT SAYS IT'S ONLY VALID FOR THE "NORMAL LENGTH OF STUDY" OF A PH.D., WHICH, ACCORDING TO THIS, IS FIVE YEARS.
JORGE CHAM © 2008
FIVE YEARS!?
SOMEONE'S BEEN FEEDING HOMELAND SECURITY FALSE INFORMATION AGAIN!
I'M HARBORING AN ILLEGAL ALIEN!?
PHEW, OK, I TALKED TO MY DSO OVER AT THE I-CENTER.
APPARENTLY, IT'S THE D/S ON THE I-20 THAT DETERMINES USCIS STATUS, NOT THE ISSUED F-1 ITSELF.
JORGE CHAM © 2008
AS LONG AS MY I-94 AND SEVIS MATCH, MY OPT IS LESS THAN 12 AND I FILED AN 8843 LAST YEAR THEN I SHOULDN'T BE DEPORTED.
...YET.
WAS THAT ENGLISH?

DOES THAT MEAN YOU CAN GO TO THE CONFERENCE?
NO, NOW I CAN'T LEAVE THE COUNTRY!
I MEAN, I COULD, BUT THEN THEY WON'T LET ME BACK IN BECAUSE MY VISA STAMP WILL BE EXPIRED.
JORGE CHAM © 2008
AND THE ONLY WAY TO GET A NEW STAMP IS TO APPLY FOR IT OUTSIDE THE COUNTRY! I'M TRAPPED!
"GIVE US YOUR TIRED, YOUR POOR, YOUR THOROUGHLY CONFUSED..."
I'M A HUDDLED MASS OF NERVES!
I'LL GO TO TIJUANA!
WHAT??
TIJUANA! I'LL CROSS THE BORDER TO MEXICO, GET MY VISA AT THE CONSULATE THERE, AND THEN BE ON LEGAL STATUS TO GO TO THE CONFERENCE NEXT WEEK!
JORGE CHAM © 2008
THAT'S CRAZY!
I'M DESPERATE!
BESIDES...
...HOW LONG CAN IT POSSIBLY TAKE?
THREE TO FOUR MONTHS!??
NEXT!

Immigration comics present:
THE F-1 STUDENT VISA PROCESS EXPLAINED
STEP →
JORGE CHAM © 2008
1 DREAM OF STUDYING IN AMERICA, LAND OF OPPORTUNITY!
technically, America is the continent...
2 FIND OUT HOW MUCH OPPORTUNITY COSTS
$$
tuition is HOW much??
3 FUTILELY WRITE TO PROFESSORS
new mail from another foreign student!
delete
4 TAKE STANDARDIZED ENGLISH TEST (years of listening to American Pop culture finally pay off!)
"a cow is a farm animal."
5 TRUST YOUR FUTURE IN HANDS OF QUESTIONABLE LOCAL MAIL SYSTEM
6 GET ACCEPTED!
i love my country!
but i can't wait to get out!

7 WAKE UP AT 4am, FORM LINE AT U.S. CONSULATE
8 GET IN, WAIT IN ANOTHER LINE
9 GET INTERVIEWED
so, what's your PhD about?
uh...
10 WAIT SOME MORE
11 VISA GRANTED!
i am a worthy human being!
12 SAY GOODBYE TO RELATIVES (THE ONES YOU LIKE)
will you come back to visit?
if i can afford it.
13 GET EYE SCANNED, FINGERPRINTED, SUBTLY INTERROGATED
so, what's your PhD about?
uh...
are you a terrorist??
14 FIND OUT UNIVERSITY IS ACTUALLY IN THE MIDDLE OF NOWHERE.
howdy, y'all!
welcome to America!
15 GET USED TO CULTURE, PAY TAXES, ESTABLISH FRIENDSHIPS
16 FACE FACT YOU ARE NOW OVER-QUALIFIED FOR MOST JOBS IN YOUR HOME COUNTRY
what is it you do again?
17 GRAPPLE WITH IDENTITY ISSUES.
who am i?
what is "home"?
18 REALIZE THE PLACE YOU NOW CALL HOME DOESN'T FEEL THE SAME WAY ABOUT YOU
what do you mean i can't get back in the country!?

THREE TO FOUR MONTHS?? THE VISA IS ONLY SUPPOSED TO TAKE A FEW HOURS!
WELL...
UNFORTUNATELY, YOUR APPLICATION TRIGGERED SEVERAL RED FLAGS IN OUR HOMELAND SECURITY DATABASE.
JORGE CHAM © 2008
YOUR COUNTRY IS ON THE "AXIS OF MISUNDERESTIMATION" BLACKLIST, YOUR TRAVEL AND INSTANT MESSAGE PATTERNS MATCH SUSPICIOUS ACTIVITY ACCORDING TO THE PHONE COMPANY. BUT WORSE OF ALL...
...YOU'RE A SOCIAL SCIENCE GRAD STUDENT IN CALIFORNIA.
WE CAN'T TAKE ANY CHANCES.
PLEASE, IF YOU DON'T APPROVE MY VISA, I'LL BE STRANDED HERE IN MEXICO!
I SUPPOSE I CAN MAKE AN EXCEPTION.
HOWEVER, YOU WILL NEED TO PROVIDE THE FOLLOWING DOCUMENTS:
1) BANK AND SALARY RECORDS THAT SHOW YOU HAVE SUFFICIENT SAVINGS AND WILL NOT BE A DRAIN ON SOCIETY...
JORGE CHAM © 2008
2) A LETTER FROM YOUR ADVISOR SAYING HOW HAPPY HE IS WITH YOUR WORK AND HOW MUCH HE SUPPORTS YOU.
AND 3) FOR SECURITY PURPOSES, A STATEMENT OF WHAT EXACTLY YOUR THESIS IS.
THOSE MIGHT BE A LITTLE DIFFICULT.
IN AMERICA, NOTHING'S TOO DIFFICULT.
NEXT!

OK, I GOT YOUR PAY STUBS AND ACCOUNT STATEMENTS FROM THE BANK...
NOW I JUST HAVE TO TRACK DOWN YOUR PROFESSOR AND GET HIS SIGNATURE ON THIS SUPPORT LETTER.
JORGE CHAM © 2008
GOSH, THANK YOU SO MUCH CECILIA... I DON'T KNOW WHAT I'D DO WITHOUT YOUR HELP..!
WELL, IT WAS THIS OR GO TO WORK TODAY.
SNIFF... AT LEAST YOU PICKED ME OVER THE INTERNET.
AH, THERE HE IS!
PROF. RIVERA!
JORGE CHAM © 2008
PROF-
PROF. RIVERA?
PROFESSORS: MORE ELUSIVE THAN NINJAS?

...I SEE HIM!
HE'S ON THE WEST CORRIDOR!
WE'VE GOT HIM CORNERED!
ALL UNITS CONVERGE! GO! GO! GO!
JORGE CHAM © 2008
SON OF A- !
OK, PEOPLE. ACCORDING TO HIS SCHEDULE, PROF. RIVERA IS CURRENTLY AT THREE DIFFERENT MEETINGS AT THE SAME TIME.
Monday
HOW IS THIS POSSIBLE?
THROUGH CAREFUL OBSERVATION, I'VE DETERMINED THAT PROFESSORS EXIST AS PROBABILITY DENSITY FUNCTIONS.
the tenure cloud
JORGE CHAM © 2008
THIS "TENURE CLOUD" OR "CLOUT" IS THE REASON WE HAVEN'T BEEN ABLE TO CATCH PROF. RIVERA AND GET HIS SIGNATURE.
WHAT IS THIS CLOUD MADE OF?
HOT AIR MOSTLY. IT'S RATHER AMBIGUOUS.
TELL ME ABOUT IT.

NINJAS vs PROFESSORS

A COMPARATIVE ANALYSIS

NINJAS	PROFESSORS
Experts in methods of subterfuge	Experts in methods no longer used
Employs assortment of lethal weapons	Employs a bunch of lazy peons (you)
Can kill you without remorse	Can kill your career or worse
Always shown wearing the same outfit	Always wears the same outfit
Wears a hood	Wears a hood at graduation
Hurls Shurikens	Hurls when you present your research
People think they're pretty cool	They think they're pretty cool
Shrouded in mystery	Shrouds you in misery

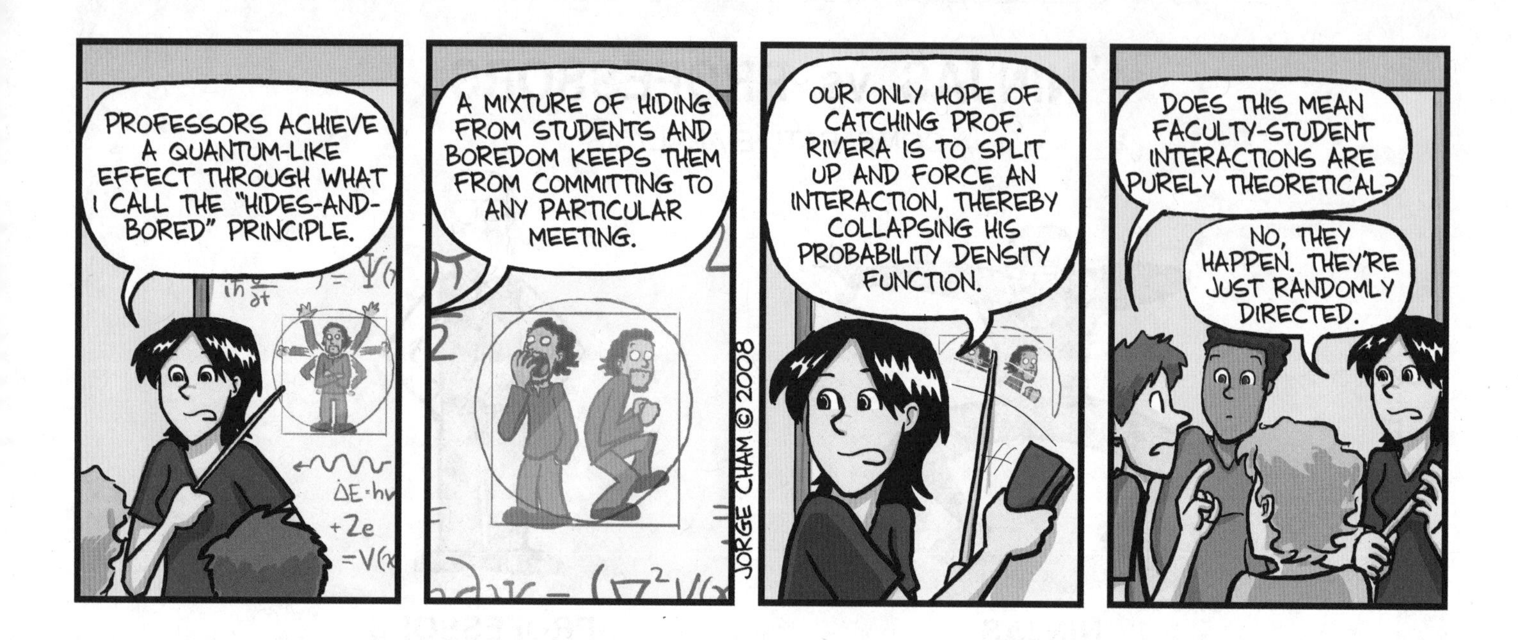
PROFESSORS ACHIEVE A QUANTUM-LIKE EFFECT THROUGH WHAT I CALL THE "HIDES-AND-BORED" PRINCIPLE.
A MIXTURE OF HIDING FROM STUDENTS AND BOREDOM KEEPS THEM FROM COMMITTING TO ANY PARTICULAR MEETING.
JORGE CHAM © 2008
OUR ONLY HOPE OF CATCHING PROF. RIVERA IS TO SPLIT UP AND FORCE AN INTERACTION, THEREBY COLLAPSING HIS PROBABILITY DENSITY FUNCTION.
DOES THIS MEAN FACULTY-STUDENT INTERACTIONS ARE PURELY THEORETICAL?
NO, THEY HAPPEN. THEY'RE JUST RANDOMLY DIRECTED.

NEGATIVE. PROFESSOR RIVERA IS NOT AT THE FACULTY MEETING.
HE'S NOT AT HIS STUDENT'S ORAL EXAM EITHER.
JORGE CHAM © 2008
WE'VE HIT ALL THE PLACES HE'S SUPPOSED TO BE AT.
WHERE COULD HE POSSIBLY BE!??
I WONDER WHAT'S GOING ON TODAY?

I'M REALLY SORRY TAJEL. PROF. RIVERA KEEPS ELUDING US!
HAVE YOU TRIED NOT NEEDING HIM?
HUH?
PROFESSORS ONLY APPEAR WHEN YOU DON'T NEED THEM.

TRY THIS: CLOSE YOUR EYES.
CONVINCE YOURSELF THAT HE'S THE LAST PERSON YOU WANT TO SEE...
I DON'T SEE HOW THIS-
DID I HEAR SOMEONE NOT NEED ME?

HERE ARE ALL THE DOCUMENTS YOU REQUESTED.
FINE, I'LL LET YOU BACK IN THE COUNTRY.
HE DIDN'T EVEN READ THEM!
SHOULD WE HEAD BACK ACROSS THE BORDER?

UH, THERE'S SOMETHING I HAVE TO DO FIRST.
WHAT IS IT?
FREE THE BURROS!
STOP TIJUANA BURRO EXPLOITATION!

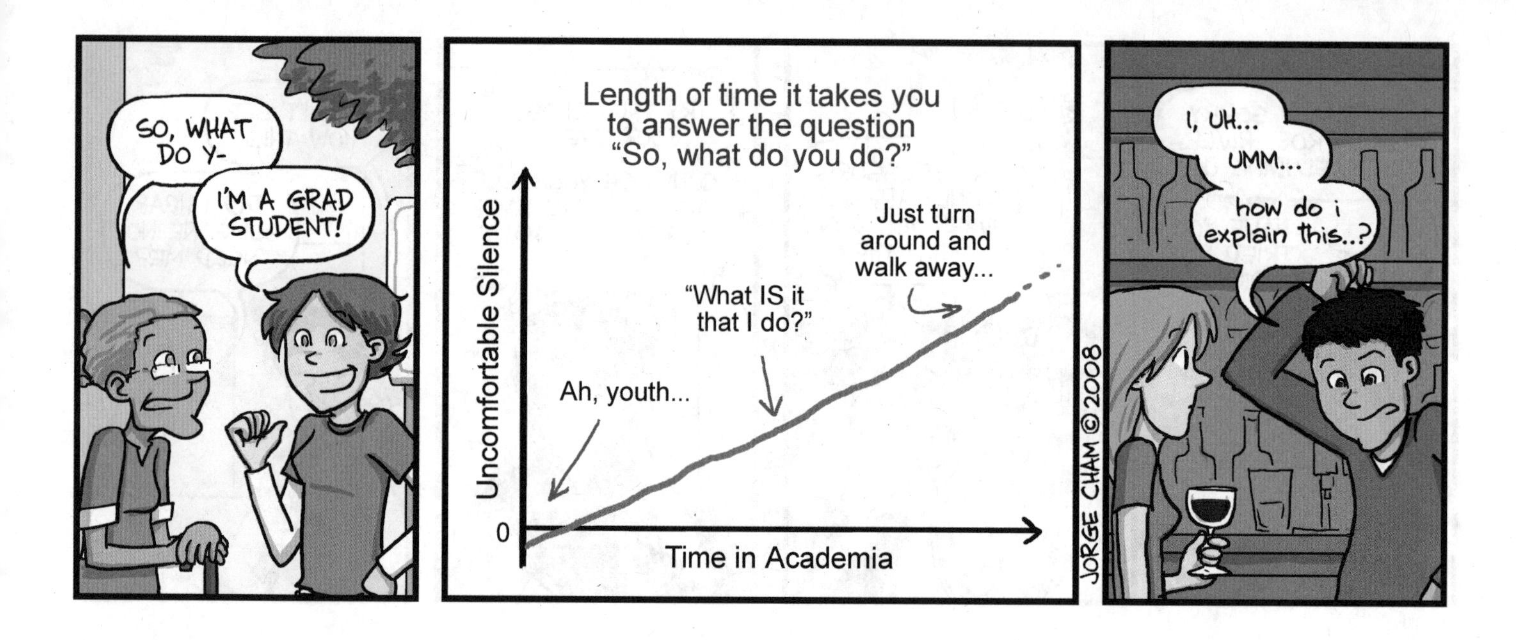

AVERAGE TIME SPENT COMPOSING ONE E-MAIL

HOW TO RUIN A GRAD STUDENT'S EVENING:
HEY, WE'RE GOING OUT FOR DRINKS. WANT TO JOIN?
GREAT.
IF I GO, I'LL SPEND THE WHOLE NIGHT FEELING GUILTY...
man, i should be working.
JORGE CHAM © 2008
IF I STAY, I'LL BE DEPRESSED ALL NIGHT FOR NOT GOING!
man, i should have gone out.
OFFER THEM A CHOICE.
THANKS A LOT!
YOU NEED HELP.

SAY, WHAT'S THE PLURAL OF "THESIS"?
IS IT "THESISES"?
"THESII"?
JORGE CHAM © 2008
"THESISISESS-ES"??
I THINK IT'S "THESES".
"THESES"? BUT THAT MEANS...
OUR DEGREES ARE MADE OF THECAL MATTER, YES.

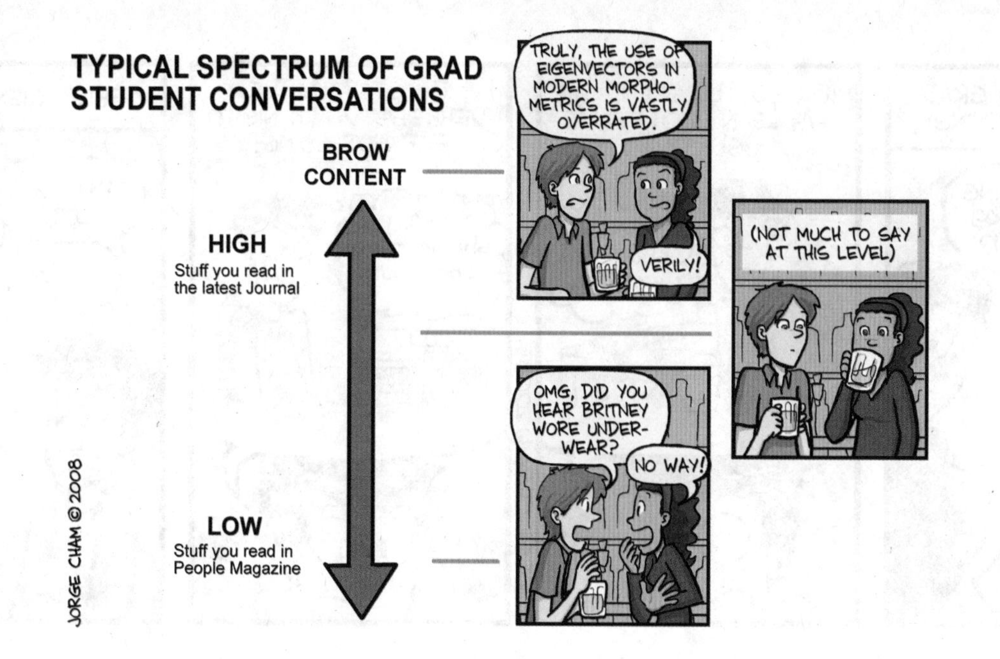
TYPICAL SPECTRUM OF GRAD STUDENT CONVERSATIONS
BROW CONTENT
HIGH
Stuff you read in the latest Journal
LOW
Stuff you read in People Magazine
TRULY, THE USE OF EIGENVECTORS IN MODERN MORPHO-METRICS IS VASTLY OVERRATED.
VERILY!
(NOT MUCH TO SAY AT THIS LEVEL)
OMG, DID YOU HEAR BRITNEY WORE UNDER-WEAR?
NO WAY!
JORGE CHAM © 2008

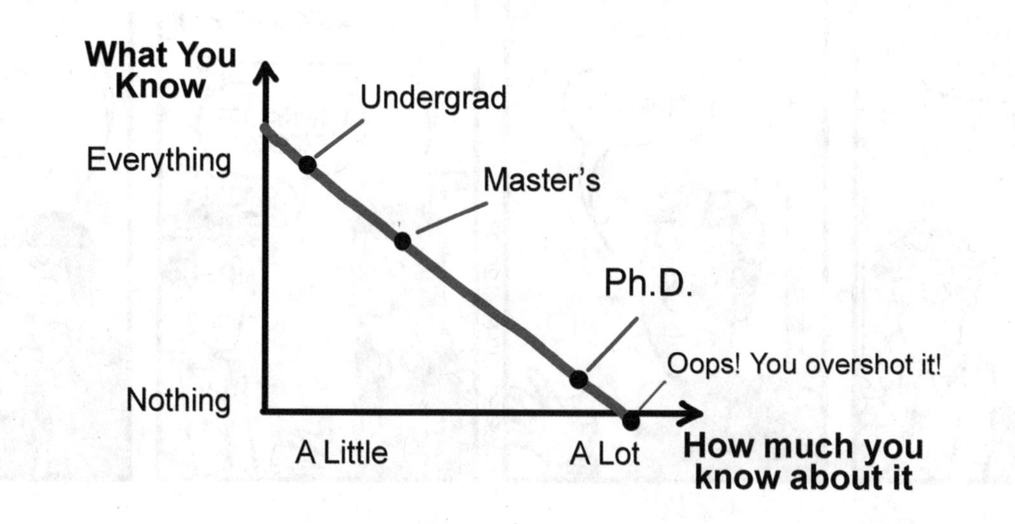
What You Know vs How much you know about it
What You Know
Everything
Nothing
Undergrad
Master's
Ph.D.
Oops! You overshot it!
A Little
A Lot
How much you know about it
JORGE CHAM © 2008

ANOTHER DAY, ANOTHER GRANT PROPOSAL.
grant submitted!
IT SEEMS ALL I EVER DO THESE DAYS IS GO TO MEETINGS AND APPLY FOR MONEY...
grant accepted!
JORGE CHAM © 2008
IS MY BRILLIANT MIND GOING TO WASTE?
IS THIS REALLY WHAT BEING A PROFESSOR IS ALL ABOUT?
THE MID-TENURE CRISIS
PERHAPS I'LL BUY MYSELF A NEW POST-DOC.

SOMETIMES I MISS THE THRILL OF HANDS-ON RESEARCH.
TO ACTUALLY DO WORK AND NOT JUST WRITE ABOUT IT OR DIRECT OTHERS TO DO IT.
JORGE CHAM © 2008
SAY, MAYBE I'LL GO DOWN TO THE LAB AND WORK AT THE BENCH FOR A WHILE.
I'M SURE THAT'LL EXCITE THE STUDENTS.
DO YOU FEEL THAT?
WHAT?
AN IMPENDING SENSE OF DOOM.

YES, I THINK SOME TIME IN THE LAB WILL DO ME GOOD.
MARY, IF ANYONE ASKS, I'LL BE DOWN IN THE LAB DOING REAL WORK.
JORGE CHAM © 2008
YOUR LAB IS THAT WAY.
RIGHT. I KNEW THAT.
!
?
JORGE CHAM © 2008
UH, HI, PROF. SMITH... WHAT ARE YOU... UM, DOING?
WHAT'S IT LOOK LIKE I'M DOING? I'M DOING RESEARCH.
ON THE MOST EXPENSIVE PIECE OF EQUIPMENT IN THE LAB?
IS THAT WHAT THIS WAS?

PROFESSOR-PROOFING YOUR WORK AREA

CREATING A SAFE ENVIRONMENT FOR YOUR ADVISOR

AH, TO WORK IN THE LAB AGAIN.
HOW I MISSED THESE EMOTIONS!
THE THRILL OF TINKERING!
THE EXCITEMENT OF EXPERIMENTATION!
FZZT!
JORGE CHAM © 2008
BOOF!
!
THE FRUSTRATION OF FAILURE...
SIGH... WHO AM I KIDDING?
I DON'T BELONG IN A LAB ANYMORE...
PERHAPS IT'S TIME I ACCEPTED THE OBVIOUS TRUTH...
JORGE CHAM © 2008
CLEARLY, THE BEST USE OF MY SUPERIOR RESEARCH SKILLS IS TELLING OTHERS HOW TO DO IT.
my thesis project!

Running...
Desktop Clean-up Wizard
Searching for unused icons on your Desktop
Unused Icons Found!
The following icons haven't been used in years:
Shortcut to Dissertation
JORGE CHAM © 2008
Delete Dissertation?
Yes
No, I will keep banging my head. Ask me again in a few years.
Warning!
System is running low on excuses. Please insert more motivation or delete unused neurons.
MAYBE I SHOULD GET A MAC.

OH, MAN, IT'S THE END OF THE DAY AND I HAVEN'T DONE ANYTHING!
THE ONLY WAY TO SALVAGE THIS IS TO COME UP WITH A SUPER BRILLIANT IDEA THAT MAKES UP FOR ALL THE TIME I WASTED.
JORGE CHAM © 2008
C'MON! BRILLIANT IDEA! BRILLIANT IDEA! THINK..!
I WONDER IF THIS IS HOW EINSTEIN CAME UP WITH E=MC²
PROBABLY NOT.

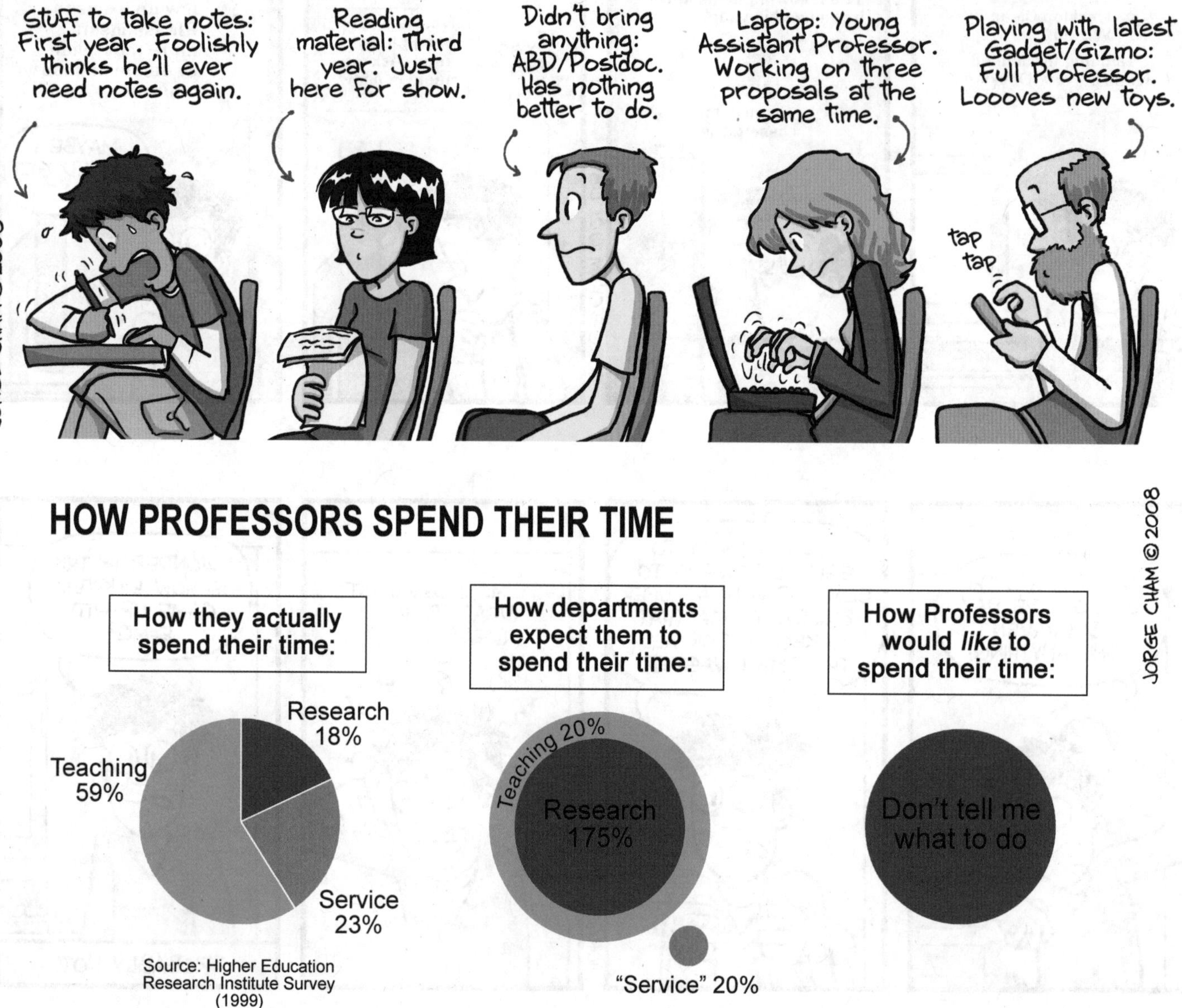
WHAT YOU BROUGHT TO SEMINAR AND WHAT IT SAYS ABOUT YOU:
Stuff to take notes: First year. Foolishly thinks he'll ever need notes again.
Reading material: Third year. Just here for show.
Didn't bring anything: ABD/Postdoc. Has nothing better to do.
Laptop: Young Assistant Professor. Working on three proposals at the same time.
Playing with latest Gadget/Gizmo: Full Professor. Loooves new toys.
tap tap
JORGE CHAM © 2008
HOW PROFESSORS SPEND THEIR TIME
How they actually spend their time:
Research 18%
Teaching 59%
Service 23%
Source: Higher Education Research Institute Survey (1999)
How departments expect them to spend their time:
Teaching 20%
Research 175%
"Service" 20%
How Professors would *like* to spend their time:
Don't tell me what to do
JORGE CHAM © 2008

Not a good sign:

$$\sigma_{t_{graduate}} > t_{graduate}$$

YEAH, I SHOULD BE DONE IN A YEAR.

PLUS OR MINUS THREE.

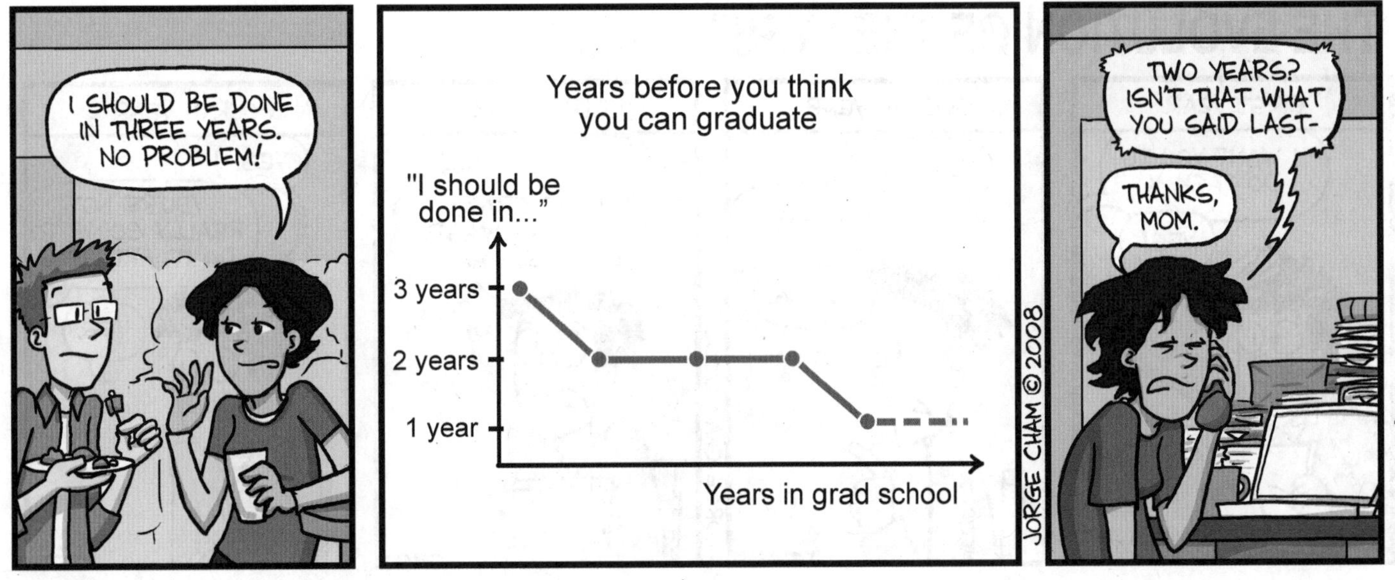

THE EVOLUTION OF THE "YES"

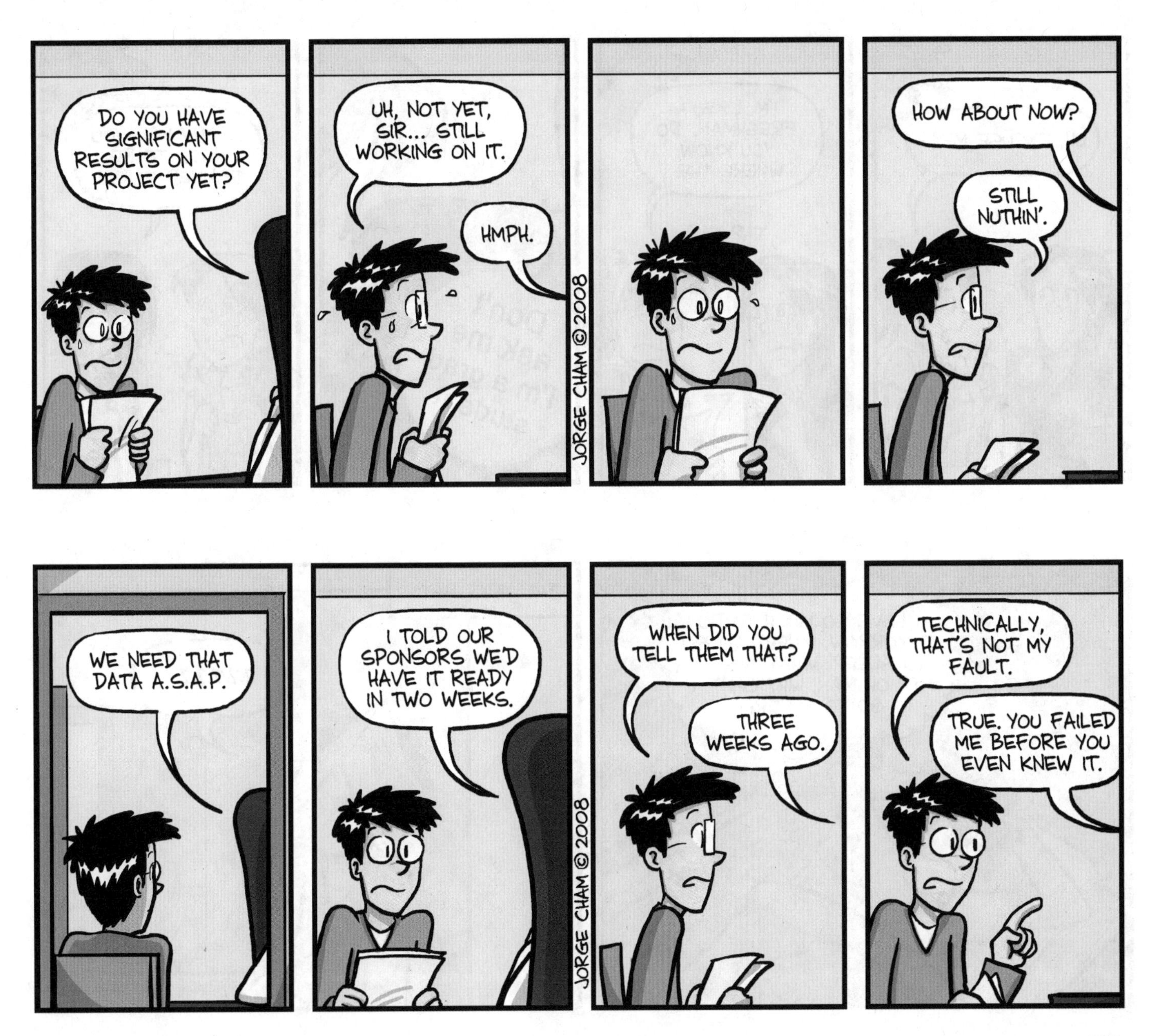

DO YOU HAVE SIGNIFICANT RESULTS ON YOUR PROJECT YET?
UH, NOT YET, SIR... STILL WORKING ON IT.
HMPH.
JORGE CHAM © 2008
HOW ABOUT NOW?
STILL NUTHIN'.
WE NEED THAT DATA A.S.A.P.
I TOLD OUR SPONSORS WE'D HAVE IT READY IN TWO WEEKS.
JORGE CHAM © 2008
WHEN DID YOU TELL THEM THAT?
THREE WEEKS AGO.
TECHNICALLY, THAT'S NOT MY FAULT.
TRUE. YOU FAILED ME BEFORE YOU EVEN KNEW IT.

UH, EXCUSE ME..?
I'M, LIKE, A FRESHMAN. DO YOU KNOW WHERE THE-
TAP TAP
JORGE CHAM © 2008
Don't ask me I'm a grad student
SORRY KID. YOU NEED TO BE TRAINED EARLY.
I HAVE SO MUCH TO DO TOMORROW. I NEED TO GO TO SLEEP. WHAT TIME IS IT? OH MAN, WHY CAN'T I GO TO SLEEP??
JORGE CHAM © 2008
THE NEXT DAY:
ZZZZZ...

I WANT YOU TO WORK ON A PET PROJECT OF MINE.
IS IT RELATED TO MY THESIS?
NOT REALLY.
JORGE CHAM © 2008
IS IT RELATED TO OUR RESEARCH AREA?
NOT BY A LONG SHOT.
DO I HAVE A CHOICE?
DO PETS?
I REALIZE IT MAY BE INAPPROPRIATE FOR ME TO ASK YOU TO DO THINGS NOT RELATED TO RESEARCH.
BUT REALLY, IT'S JUST COST EFFICIENT.
JORGE CHAM © 2008
IF YOU DO MY MENIAL TASKS FOR ME, I HAVE MORE TIME TO WORK ON RESEARCH, WHICH BENEFITS YOU INDIRECTLY.
BUT THEN I DON'T GET ANY WORK DONE.
EXACTLY. YOU HAVE NOTHING TO LOSE.

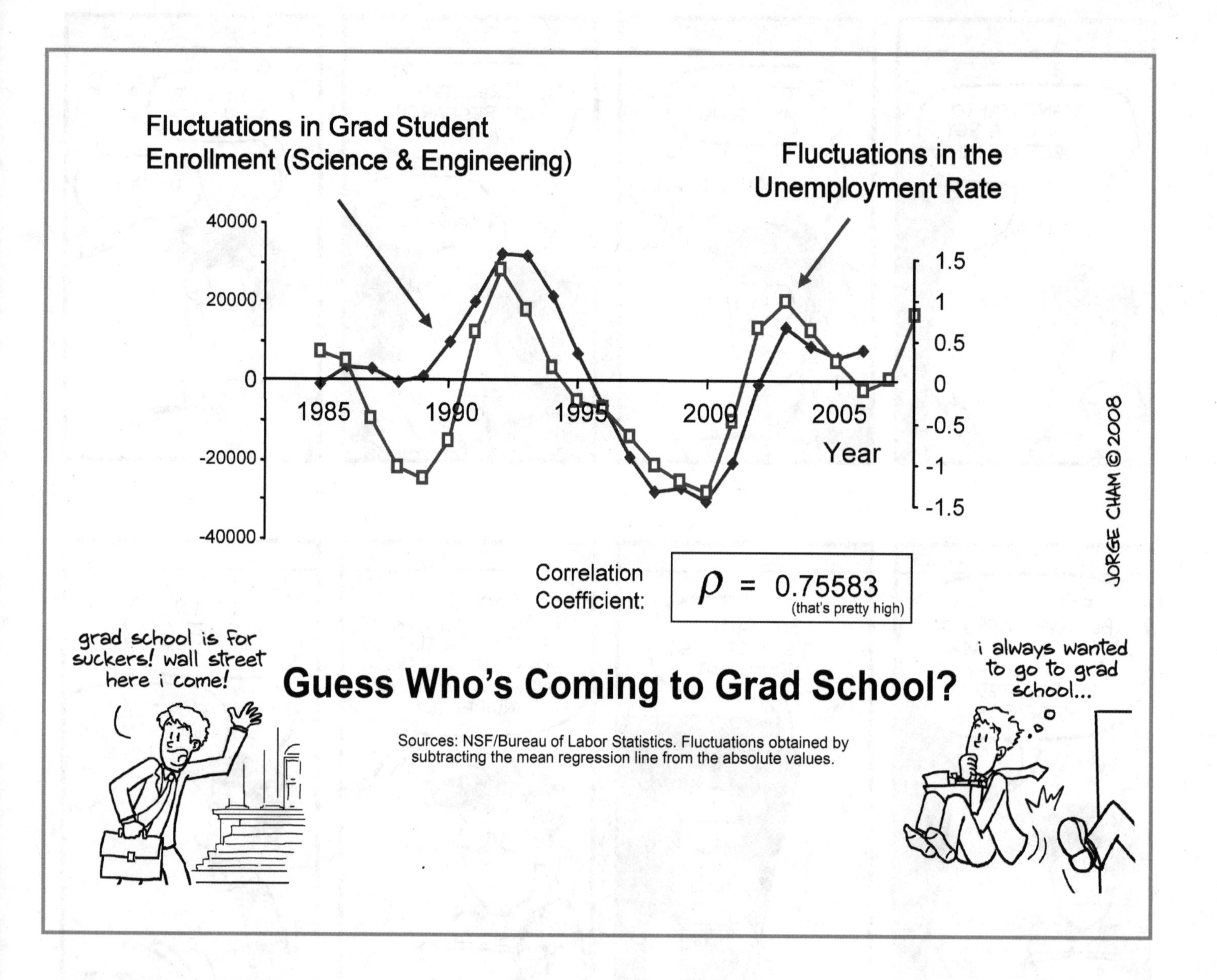
Fluctuations in Grad Student Enrollment (Science & Engineering)
Fluctuations in the Unemployment Rate
40000
20000
0
-20000
-40000
1985
1990
1995
2000
2005
Year
1.5
1
0.5
0
-0.5
-1
-1.5
JORGE CHAM © 2008
Correlation Coefficient:
ρ = 0.75583
(that's pretty high)
grad school is for suckers! wall street here i come!
Guess Who's Coming to Grad School?
i always wanted to go to grad school...
Sources: NSF/Bureau of Labor Statistics. Fluctuations obtained by subtracting the mean regression line from the absolute values.

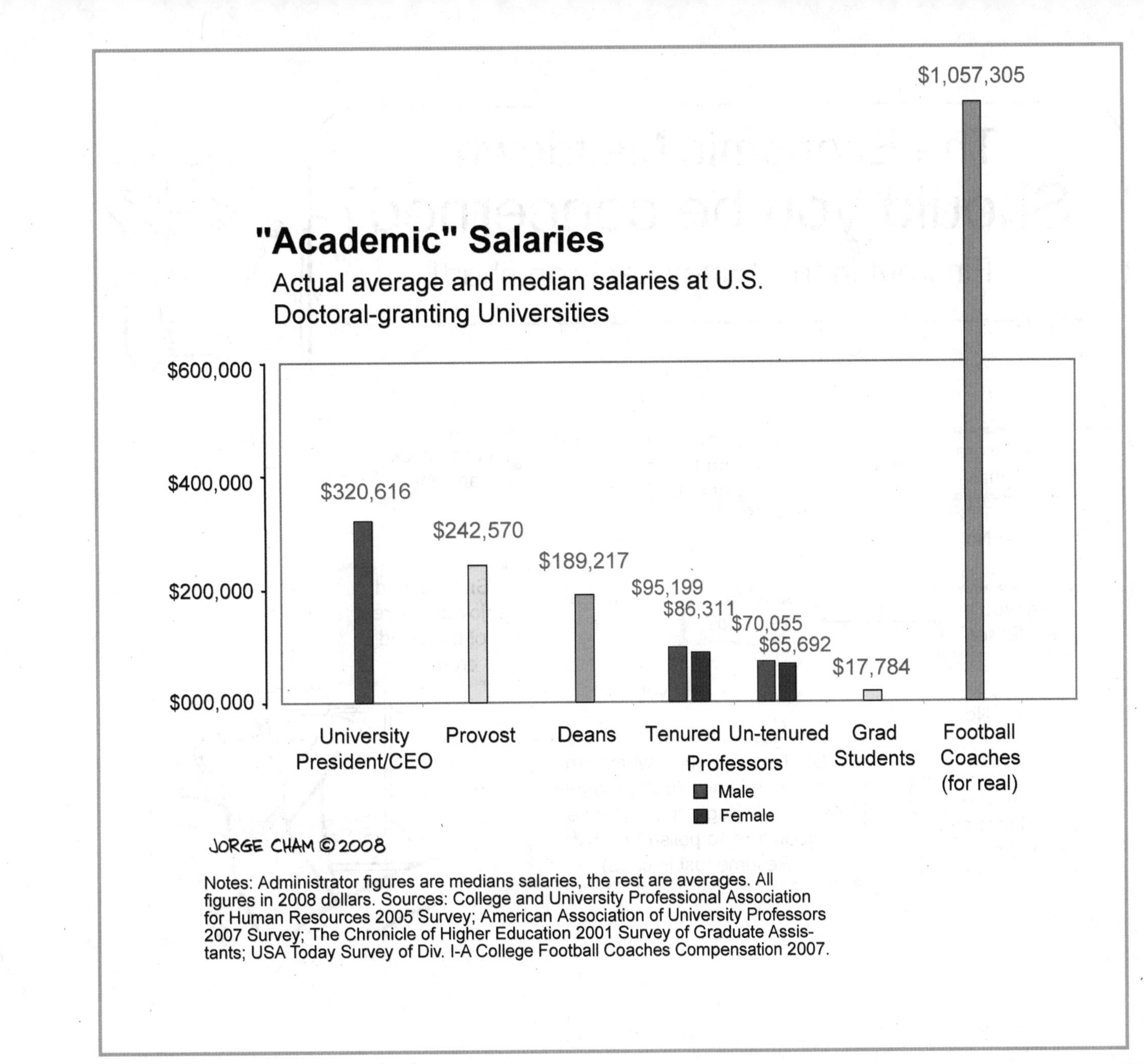
"Academic" Salaries
Actual average and median salaries at U.S. Doctoral-granting Universities
$600,000
$400,000
$200,000
$000,000
$320,616
$242,570
$189,217
$95,199
$86,311
$70,055
$65,692
$17,784
$1,057,305
University President/CEO
Provost
Deans
Tenured
Un-tenured
Professors
Male
Female
Grad Students
Football Coaches (for real)
JORGE CHAM © 2008
Notes: Administrator figures are medians salaries, the rest are averages. All figures in 2008 dollars. Sources: College and University Professional Association for Human Resources 2005 Survey; American Association of University Professors 2007 Survey; The Chronicle of Higher Education 2001 Survey of Graduate Assistants; USA Today Survey of Div. I-A College Football Coaches Compensation 2007.

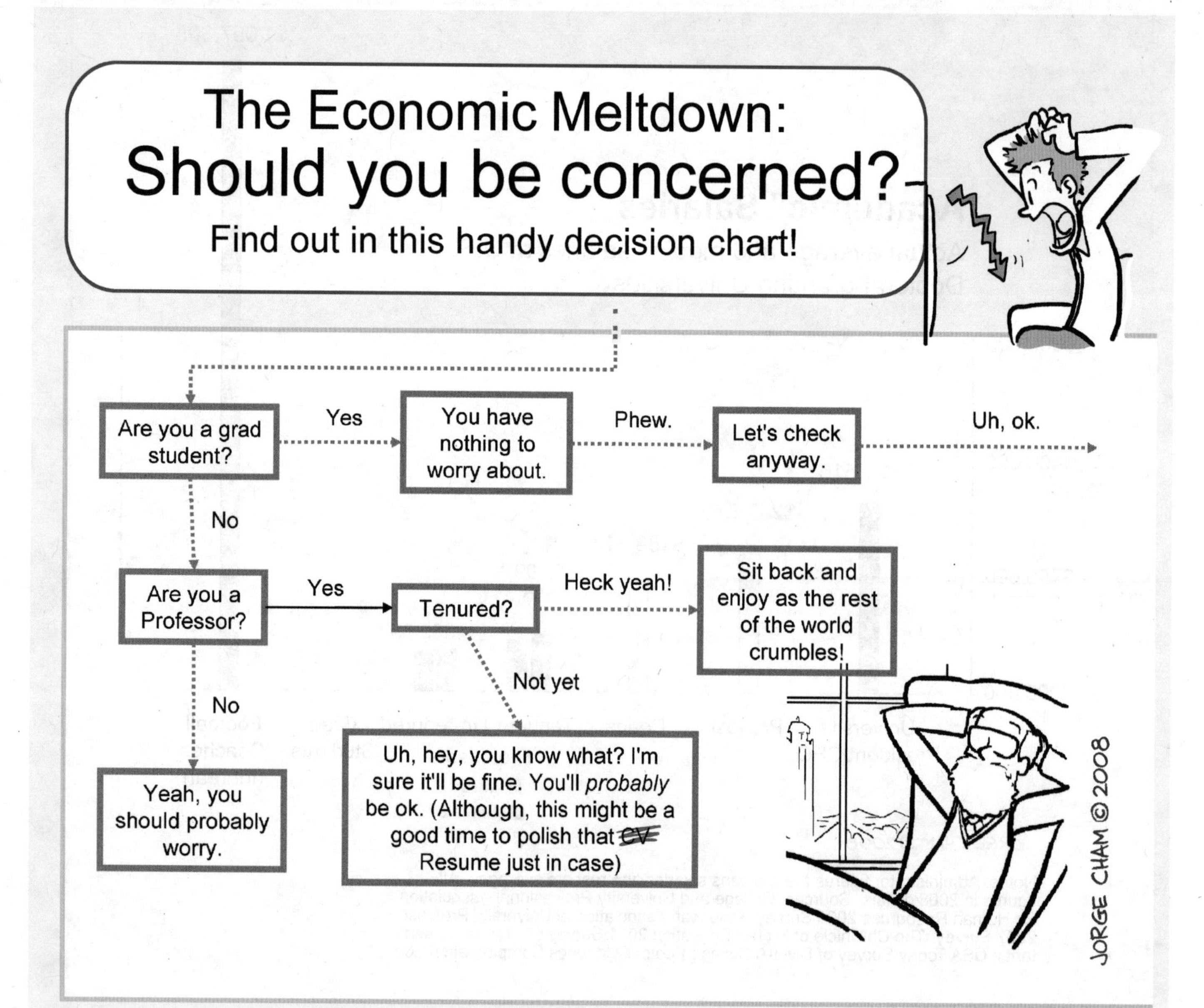
The Economic Meltdown:
Should you be concerned?
Find out in this handy decision chart!
Are you a grad student?
Yes
You have nothing to worry about.
Phew.
Let's check anyway.
Uh, ok.
No
Are you a Professor?
Yes
Tenured?
Heck yeah!
Sit back and enjoy as the rest of the world crumbles!
Not yet
No
Yeah, you should probably worry.
Uh, hey, you know what? I'm sure it'll be fine. You'll *probably* be ok. (Although, this might be a good time to polish that ~~CV~~ Resume just in case)
JORGE CHAM © 2008

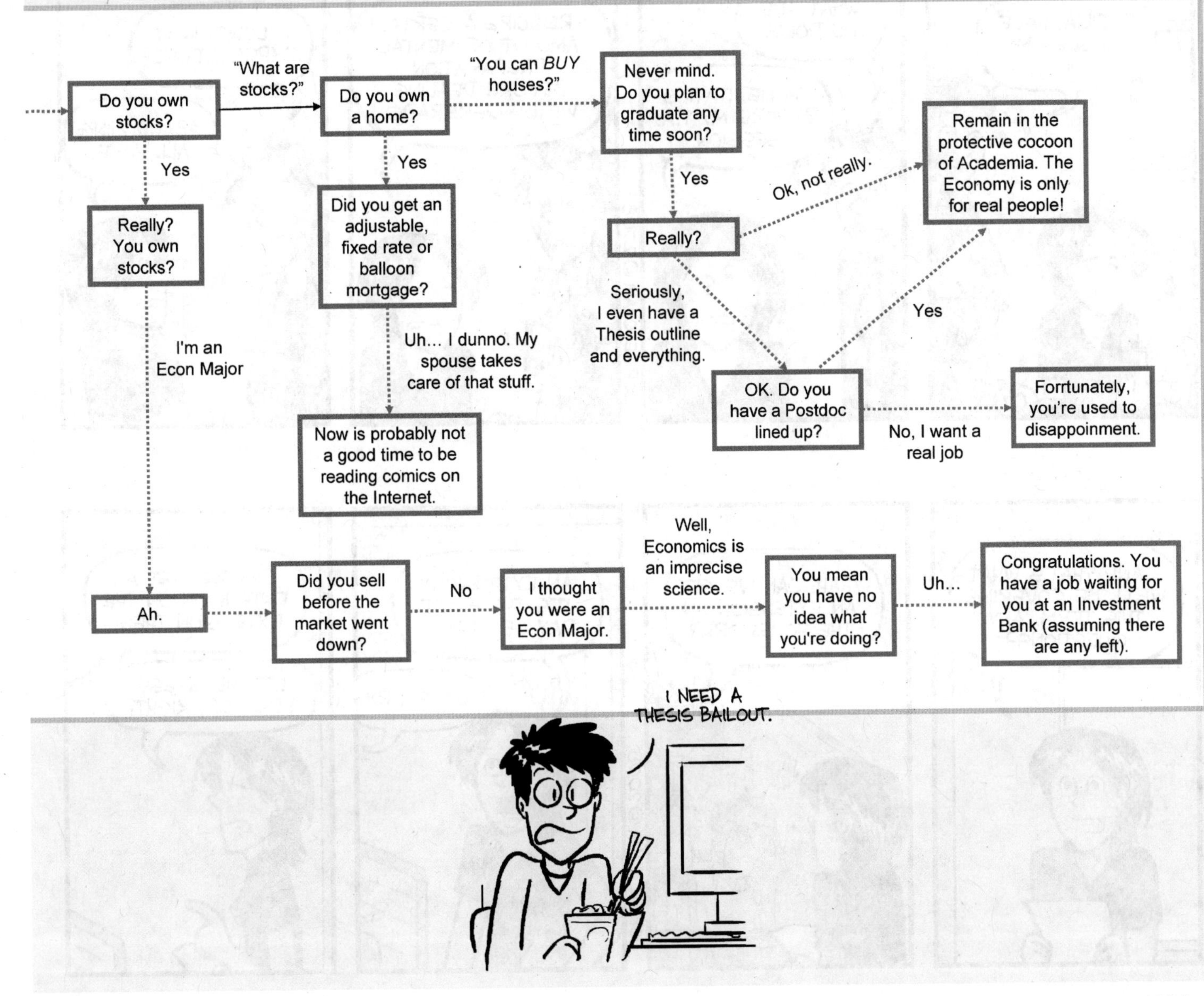
Do you own stocks?
"What are stocks?"
Do you own a home?
"You can *BUY* houses?"
Never mind. Do you plan to graduate any time soon?
Remain in the protective cocoon of Academia. The Economy is only for real people!
Yes
Really? You own stocks?
Yes
Did you get an adjustable, fixed rate or balloon mortgage?
Yes
Really?
Ok, not really.
Seriously, I even have a Thesis outline and everything.
Yes
I'm an Econ Major
Uh... I dunno. My spouse takes care of that stuff.
Now is probably not a good time to be reading comics on the Internet.
OK. Do you have a Postdoc lined up?
No, I want a real job
Forrtunately, you're used to disappointment.
Ah.
Did you sell before the market went down?
No
I thought you were an Econ Major.
Well, Economics is an imprecise science.
You mean you have no idea what you're doing?
Uh...
Congratulations. You have a job waiting for you at an Investment Bank (assuming there are any left).
I NEED A THESIS BAILOUT.

CECILIA, HAVE YOU SEEN MY- OH.
WHAT ARE YOU DOING?
I'M MEDITATING BEFORE MY T.A. SESSION.
JORGE CHAM © 2008
I REQUIRE A CERTAIN AMOUNT OF MENTAL PREPARATION BEFORE DEALING WITH UNDERGRADS.
LOWERING EXPECTATIONS?
ABANDONING ALL HOPE.
...AND THAT'S WHAT WE'LL BE COVERING THIS TERM. ANY QUESTIONS?
YEAH, CAN WE GET AN EXTENSION ON THE HOMEWORK?
JORGE CHAM © 2008
AN EXTENSION? IT'S THE FIRST DAY OF CLASS!
UH, SORRY.
CAN WE GET AN EXTENSION ON THE EXTENSION THEN?
LET ME GUESS: PRE-MED, RIGHT?

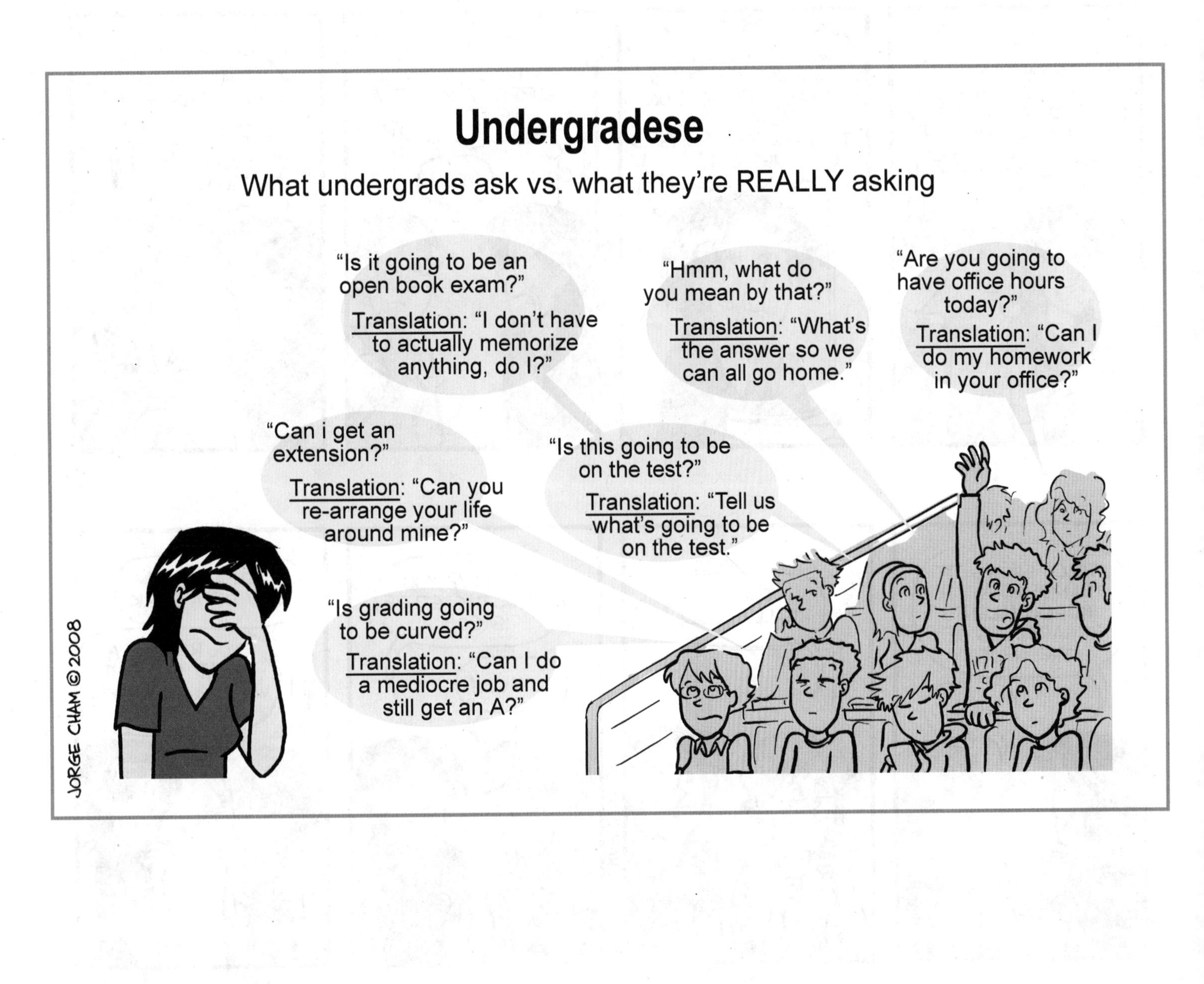
Undergradese
What undergrads ask vs. what they're REALLY asking
"Can i get an extension?" Translation: "Can you re-arrange your life around mine?"
"Is it going to be an open book exam?" Translation: "I don't have to actually memorize anything, do I?"
"Is this going to be on the test?" Translation: "Tell us what's going to be on the test."
"Hmm, what do you mean by that?" Translation: "What's the answer so we can all go home."
"Are you going to have office hours today?" Translation: "Can I do my homework in your office?"
"Is grading going to be curved?" Translation: "Can I do a mediocre job and still get an A?"
JORGE CHAM © 2008

UH OH. HERE COMES AN UNDER-GRAD TO ASK ME A QUESTION.
WHAT'S IT GOING TO BE? HER COMPUTER CRASHED? HER DOG FAINTED? THE HOMEWORK BUMS HER OUT?
JORGE CHAM © 2008
NOTHING WOULD SURPRISE ME AT THIS POINT...
YES?
THAT CLASS WAS AWESOME!
EXCEPT THAT.
...WHICH SHOWS THE TRANSFORMATION IS EQUIVALENT REGARDLESS OF THE INPUT.
WHOA...
THAT'S REALLY COOL!
JORGE CHAM © 2008
REALLY? YOU THINK THIS STUFF IS COOL?
TOTALLY!
THEN AGAIN, I'M KIND OF A DORK.
YOU'RE LIKE A GRAD STUDENT WAITING TO HAPPEN, AREN'T YOU?

OH MAN, I CAN'T WAIT 'TIL WE GET TO THE MORE COMPLICATED STUFF.
WELL, THANKS FOR ANSWERING MY QUESTIONS!
BYE!
JORGE CHAM © 2008
SEE YOU NEXT WEEK!
REASONS FOR T.A.ing:
PAYS THE BILLS.
LOOKS GOOD ON C.V.
THE ONE UNDERGRAD WHO CARES

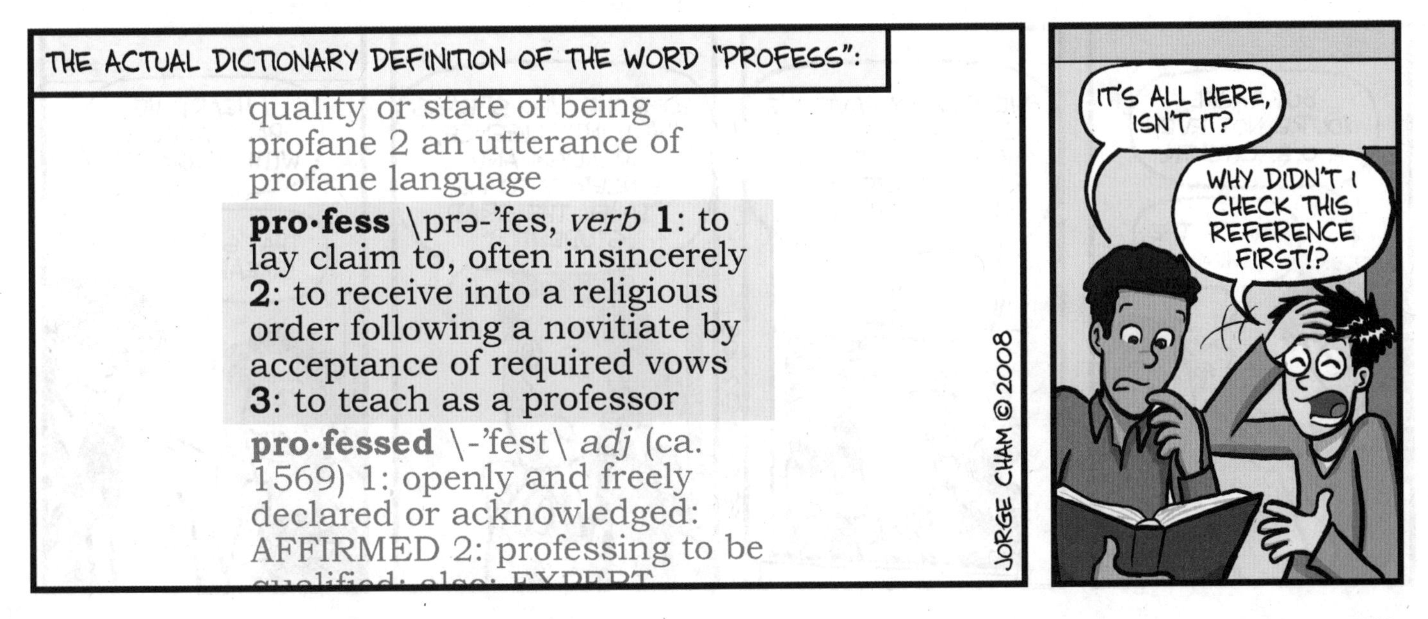
THE ACTUAL DICTIONARY DEFINITION OF THE WORD "PROFESS":
quality or state of being profane 2 an utterance of profane language
pro·fess \prə-'fes, verb 1: to lay claim to, often insincerely 2: to receive into a religious order following a novitiate by acceptance of required vows 3: to teach as a professor
pro·fessed \-'fest\ adj (ca. 1569) 1: openly and freely declared or acknowledged: AFFIRMED 2: professing to be
JORGE CHAM © 2008
IT'S ALL HERE, ISN'T IT?
WHY DIDN'T I CHECK THIS REFERENCE FIRST!?

TAJEL? HAVE YOU BEEN AT THE COMPUTER ALL DAY?
IT'S... IT'S THE ELECTION!
I CAN'T STOP CHECKING THE NEWS!
RELOAD RELOAD
JORGE CHAM © 2008
I'M SO AFRAID OF WHAT CAN HAPPEN THESE LAST FEW WEEKS, I'M OBSESSED WITH ALL THE CAMPAIGN MINUTIAE..!
WHAT ABOUT YOUR RESEARCH?
IT'S SUSPENDED. APPARENTLY, YOU CAN DO THAT.
BUT TAJEL, YOU'RE NOT EVEN A U.S. CITIZEN.
THAT'S THE THING!
WE FINALLY HAVE THE CHANCE TO ELECT A WORLD LEADER WHO REALIZES WE'RE ALL IN THIS TOGETHER...
JORGE CHAM © 2008
SOMEONE WHO SPEAKS WITH INTELLIGENCE, IDEALISM AND SINCERITY TO ME, "TAJEL THE GRAD STUDENT"™
I HEARD HE PALS AROUND WITH THEORISTS.
THAT'S A SMEAR!

THE POST-ELECTION HIGH:
JORGE CHAM © 2008
I FEEL GREAT!
I HAVEN'T BEEN THIS OPTIMISTIC ABOUT LIFE SINCE... SINCE...
HAS IT BEEN THAT LONG??
...BEFORE YOU STARTED GRAD SCHOOL?
What your Vote Helps Determine
JORGE CHAM © 2008
In Millions of Dollars
Bush
Clinton
more Bush
9,000,000
7,000,000
5,000,000
80,000
70,000
60,000
50,000
40,000
30,000
20,000
10,000
0
160
150
140
1988
1992
1996
2000
2004
2008
The National Debt
Federal Research Funding for:
National Defense
Health
Space research and technology
General science and basic research
Natural resources and environment
Energy
National Endowment for the Humanities
WHAT ABOUT 9/11?
WHAT ABOUT IT?
Sources: National Debt data from the Treasury Department. Federal funding by function from NSF. NEH budget data from NEH via National Assemblies of State Arts Agencies. All figures adjusted for inflation and shown in 2008 dollars.

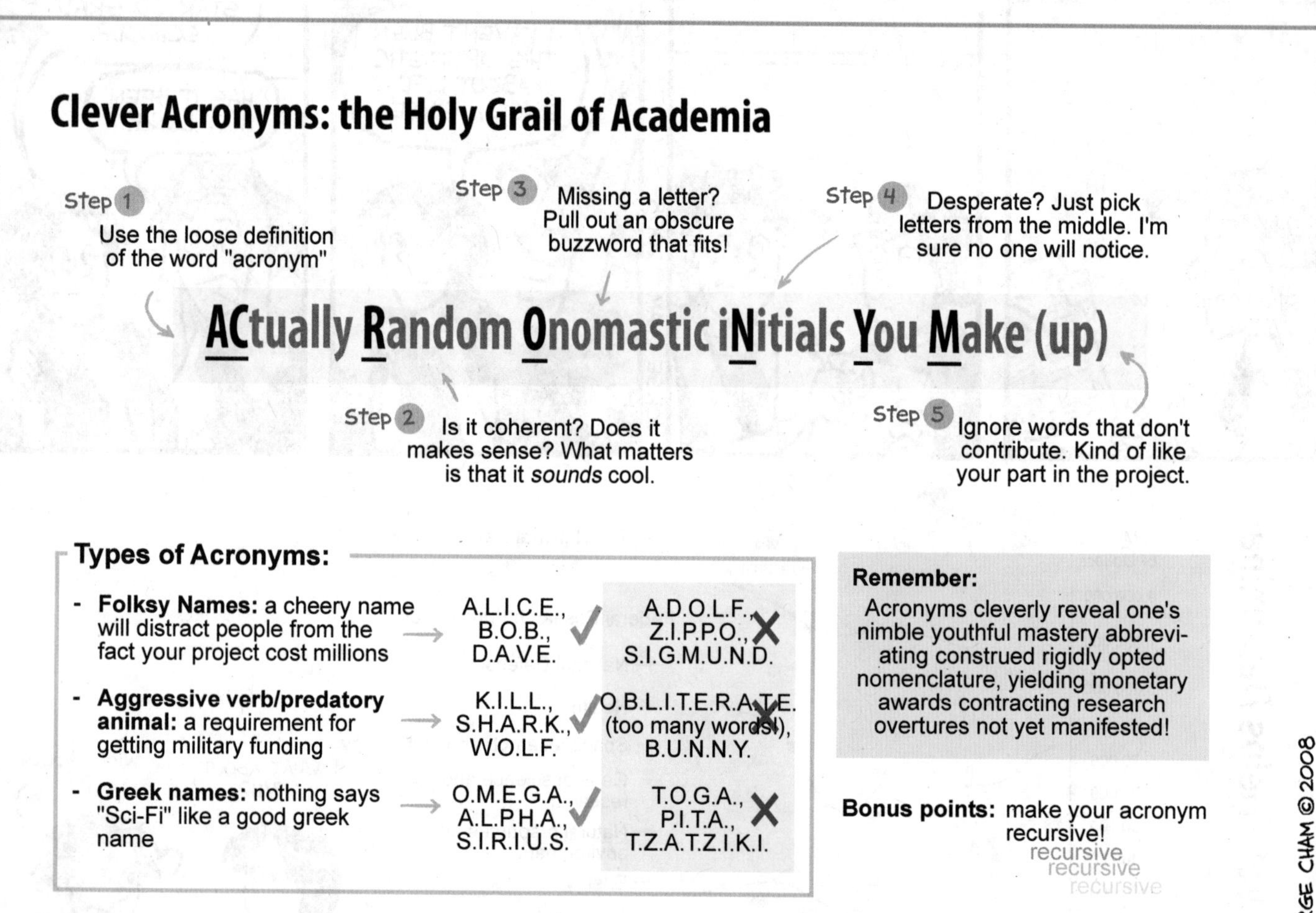
Clever Acronyms: the Holy Grail of Academia
Step 1 Use the loose definition of the word "acronym"
Step 3 Missing a letter? Pull out an obscure buzzword that fits!
Step 4 Desperate? Just pick letters from the middle. I'm sure no one will notice.
ACtually Random Onomastic iNitials You Make (up)
Step 2 Is it coherent? Does it makes sense? What matters is that it sounds cool.
Step 5 Ignore words that don't contribute. Kind of like your part in the project.
Types of Acronyms:
- Folksy Names: a cheery name will distract people from the fact your project cost millions
A.L.I.C.E., B.O.B., D.A.V.E.
A.D.O.L.F., Z.I.P.P.O., S.I.G.M.U.N.D.
- Aggressive verb/predatory animal: a requirement for getting military funding
K.I.L.L., S.H.A.R.K., W.O.L.F.
O.B.L.I.T.E.R.A.T.E. (too many words!), B.U.N.N.Y.
- Greek names: nothing says "Sci-Fi" like a good greek name
O.M.E.G.A., A.L.P.H.A., S.I.R.I.U.S.
T.O.G.A., P.I.T.A., T.Z.A.T.Z.I.K.I.
Remember:
Acronyms cleverly reveal one's nimble youthful mastery abbreviating construed rigidly opted nomenclature, yielding monetary awards contracting research overtures not yet manifested!
Bonus points: make your acronym recursive!
recursive
recursive
recursive
JORGE CHAM © 2008

How long your Prof. thinks it should take to do something		How long it'll actually take you to do it
"Trivial"	=	There goes your week.
"Easy enough"	=	Pull your hair out for a month.
"About a week"	=	Actually, this is pretty easy. He/she doesn't know there's technology that will do this for you now. Take the week off!
"Should keep you occupied for the rest of the term"	=	He/she will forget they asked you to do this by the end of the term. Don't even bother.
"This might make a good thesis topic"	=	Say hello to your thesis topic.
"Hmmm..."	=	Uh oh.

I NEED YOUR HELP, CECILIA.
I'M WRITING A GRANT PROPOSAL AND I WANT TO INCLUDE A SECTION ON THE WORK THAT YOU DO.
JORGE CHAM © 2008
SURE, DR. JONES. DO YOU NEED A FIGURE OR REFERENCE FROM ME?
I NEED TO KNOW WHAT IT IS YOU DO.
SERIOUSLY, I HAVE NO IDEA.
AND YOU THINK I DO?
PROF. JONES, I'M SHOCKED YOU DON'T KNOW WHAT MY RESEARCH IS ABOUT!
OF COURSE I DO!
I MEAN, I HAVE A GENERAL IDEA OF WHAT YOU'RE WORKING ON...
JORGE CHAM © 2008
ROUGHLY SPEAKING, I HAVE A VAGUE OVERALL SENSE OF THE THEMATIC DIRECTION OF WHAT YOU'RE BROADLY TRYING TO ACCOMPLISH.
REALLY? WHAT WAS MY LAST PAPER ABOUT?
YOU KNOW. STUFF.

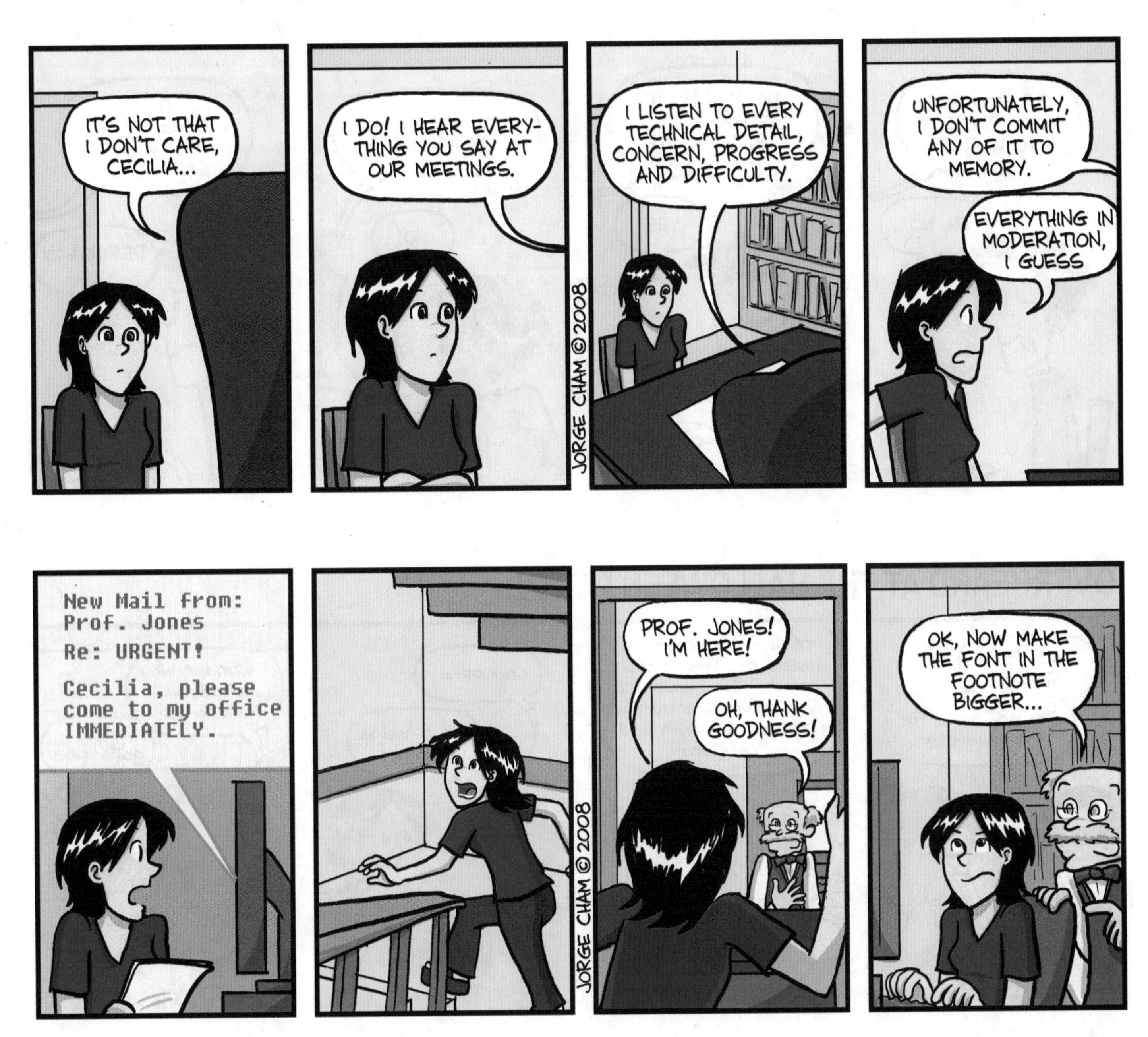
IT'S NOT THAT I DON'T CARE, CECILIA...
I DO! I HEAR EVERYTHING YOU SAY AT OUR MEETINGS.
JORGE CHAM © 2008
I LISTEN TO EVERY TECHNICAL DETAIL, CONCERN, PROGRESS AND DIFFICULTY.
UNFORTUNATELY, I DON'T COMMIT ANY OF IT TO MEMORY.
EVERYTHING IN MODERATION, I GUESS
New Mail from: Prof. Jones
Re: URGENT!
Cecilia, please come to my office IMMEDIATELY.
JORGE CHAM © 2008
PROF. JONES! I'M HERE!
OH, THANK GOODNESS!
OK, NOW MAKE THE FONT IN THE FOOTNOTE BIGGER...

OVERHEARD AT THE HALLOWEEN PARTY

WHAT'S WITH THOSE PEOPLE STANDING THERE?
WHAT PEOPLE?
JORGE CHAM © 2008
THEM! RIGHT THERE!
I DON'T SEE ANYBODY.
I... I SEE GHOSTS!
ACTUALLY, WE'RE POSTDOCS.
YES, POSTDOCS ARE THE INVISIBLE PEOPLE ON CAMPUS.
WITHOUT OFFICIAL STATUS, WE WANDER AROUND LIKE GHOSTS...
JORGE CHAM © 2008
TRAPPED IN THIS REALITY UNTIL WE'RE CALLED ON TO THE NEXT WORLD!
I THOUGHT GRAD SCHOOL WAS LIMBO.
THERE'S ANOTHER ONE AFTER THAT.

WE'RE ALL JUST WAITING FOR OUR GOLDEN TICKET OUT OF HERE.
i got a Faculty job!
UNTIL THEN, WE'RE STUCK HERE AS POSTDOCS.
JORGE CHAM © 2008
HOW LONG DOES A POSTDOC LAST?
ABOUT TWO YEARS...
THAT'S NOT BA-
...EACH.
THIS IS MY SIXTH POSTDOC.
SO HOW COME THEY CAN STILL SEE ME?
who are you talking to?
I DON'T KNOW... PERHAPS SOMETHING IS HOLDING YOU BACK FROM BEING A FULL POSTDOC...
JORGE CHAM © 2008
WAS YOUR THESIS APPROVED?
YES.
DID YOU PAY ALL THE EXIT FEES TO GRADUATE?
I THINK SO.
WHAT DID YOU HAVE FOR LUNCH?
RAMEN.
THAT'S PROBABLY IT.

YOU SEE, GRAD STUDENTS LOOK AT POSTDOCS THE SAME WAY UNDERGRADS LOOK AT GRAD STUDENTS...
...WITH A MIXTURE OF PITY AND INCOMPREHENSION.
JORGE CHAM © 2008
TO THEM, WE'RE JUST OLD PEOPLE WITH QUESTIONABLE CAREER CHOICES.
SO AS A POSTDOC, I HAVE TO HATE GRAD STUDENTS NOW?
NAH, JUST YOURSELF.
YOU'RE SAYING I'M GOING TO TURN INVISIBLE?
I'LL BE SO IGNORED AS A POSTDOC, IT'S LIKE I WON'T EVEN BE THERE?
I'M AFRAID SO.
JORGE CHAM © 2008
I'LL BE RIGHT BACK.
EXCUSE ME.
I'M INVISIBLE!!

New Mail from:
Prof. Jones
Re: Your progress report
Cecilia,
I spent nearly an hour preparing a detailed response offering sugges- tions for each of the problems you presented in your progress report.
JORGE CHAM © 2008
However, it appears I once again hit the 'delete' button instead of the 'send' button and lost the e-mail.
Unfortunately, I don't remember what I wrote. By the way, we need to finish this project SOON.
-Prof. Jones
thunk.
thunk.

THE PAPER DRAFT YOU SUBMITTED TO ME IS COMPLETELY UNACCEPTABLE.
THE WRITING IS TERRIBLE!
JUST LOOK AT THIS SENTENCE HERE! IT'S-
JORGE CHAM © 2008
HMM, NOW THAT I ACTUALLY READ IT, IT'S NOT THAT BAD.
NEXT TIME, TRY TO BE GOOD THE FIRST TIME I SKIM OVER YOUR WORK.

To all University employees,
Due to the economic situation, and the resulting reduction in endowment income (yes, we've been gambling it on the stock market)...
...the University will schedule a series of unpaid leave days for all employees (the "leave" part only applies to staff, not faculty or postdocs).
JORGE CHAM © 2008
Grad students, we are happy to announce, are exempt from such measures.
They' re so cheap, it wouldn't make a difference anyway. Happy Holidays!
- Office of the President

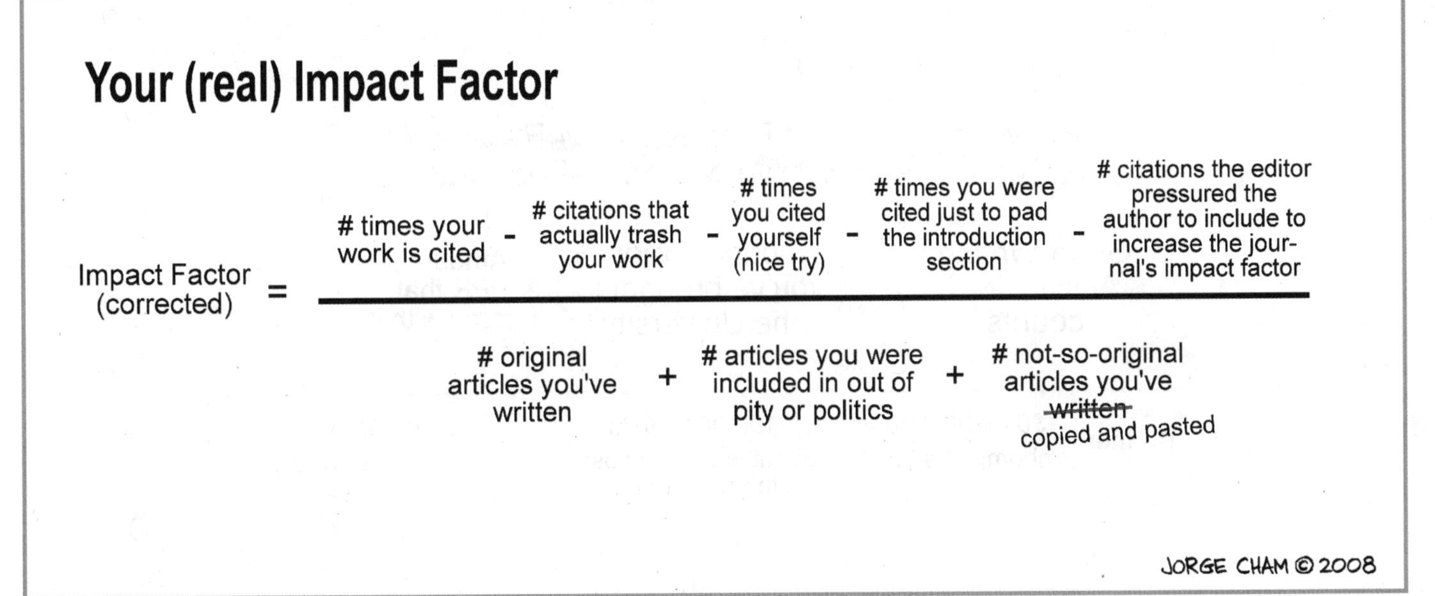
Your (real) Impact Factor
Impact Factor (corrected)
=
times your work is cited
-
citations that actually trash your work
-
times you cited yourself (nice try)
-
times you were cited just to pad the introduction section
-
citations the editor pressured the author to include to increase the journal's impact factor
original articles you've written
+
articles you were included in out of pity or politics
+
not-so-original articles you've ~~written~~ copied and pasted
JORGE CHAM © 2008

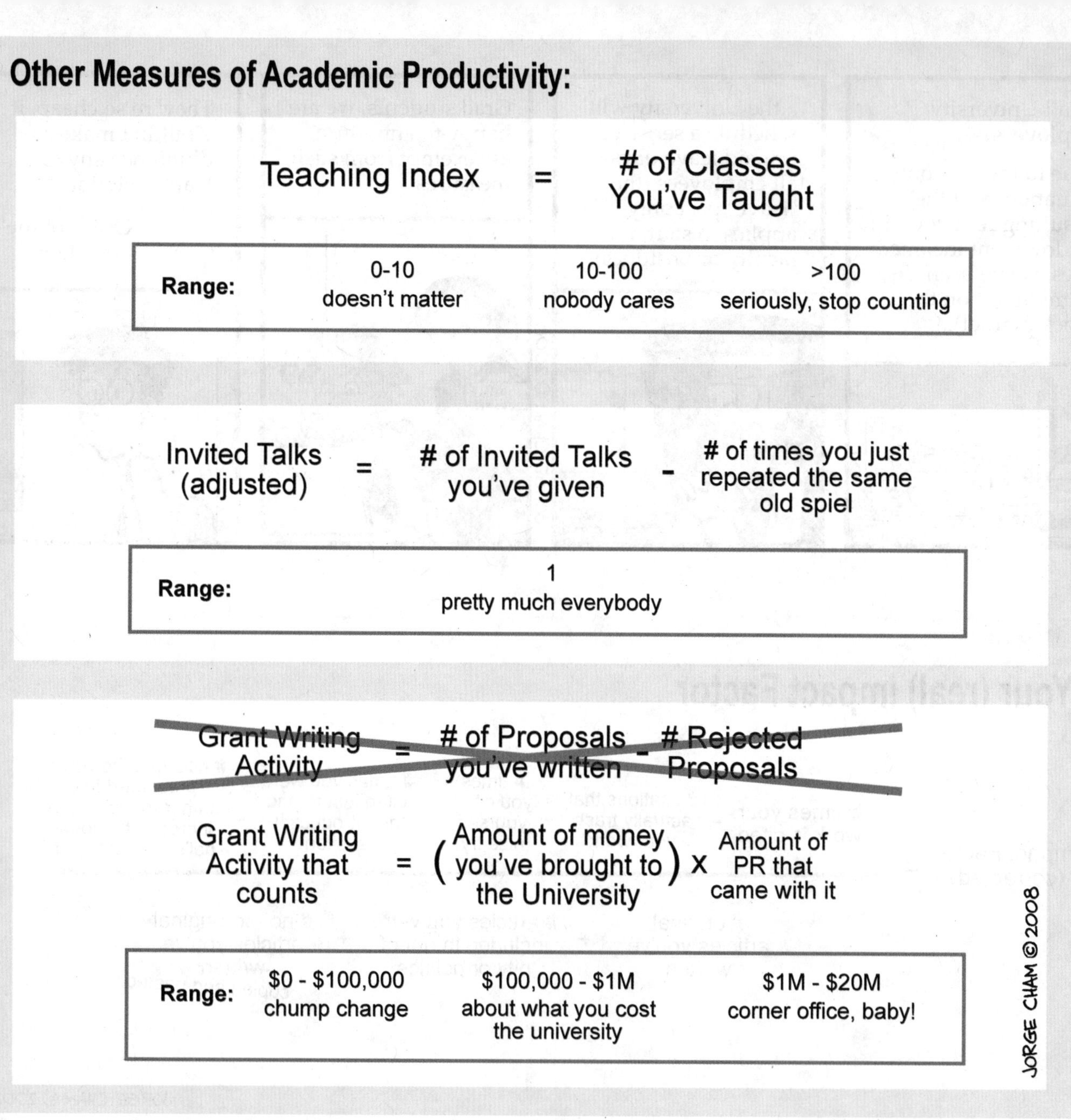
Other Measures of Academic Productivity:
Teaching Index = # of Classes You've Taught
Range:
0-10 doesn't matter
10-100 nobody cares
>100 seriously, stop counting
Invited Talks (adjusted) = # of Invited Talks you've given - # of times you just repeated the same old spiel
Range:
1 pretty much everybody
Grant Writing Activity = # of Proposals you've written - # Rejected Proposals
Grant Writing Activity that counts = (Amount of money you've brought to the University) x Amount of PR that came with it
Range:
$0 - $100,000 chump change
$100,000 - $1M about what you cost the university
$1M - $20M corner office, baby!
JORGE CHAM © 2008

Abstract MadLibs!!

This paper presents a __________ (synonym for *new*) method for __________ (sciencey verb) the __________________ (noun few people have heard of). Using ________________ (something you didn't invent), the ___________ (property) was measured to be ______ (number) +/- _______ (number) _______ (units). Results show _____________ (sexy adjective) agreement with theoretical predictions and significant improvement over previous efforts by ___________ (Loser), et al. The work presented here has profound implications for future studies of ______________ (buzzword) and may one day help solve the problem of _________________________ (supreme sociological concern).

Keywords: ____________ (buzzword), ______________ (buzzword), _____________ (buzzword)

A Christmas Song
(PhD Version)

First years roasting over Qualifiers...
Mean Profs ripping up their notes
Old-time papers, being read, lest required
and folks stressed out from Pass/Fail votes

Everybody knows that deadlines for professor jobs
Are due at end of season Fall...
So Post-docs, with their eyes filled with sobs
will find it hard to sleep at all

You know that old age is on its way...
you're lacking lots of dough and goodies in your pay
And every worried mother's gonna wish
...to see if you'll ever really finish!

And so, we're offering this comic strip
to Grads of years from nine to two......
Although it's been said, that you're atheist
Merry Christmas, poor you..!

NOT FEELING OPTIMISTIC ABOUT THE FUTURE?
I GUESS I'VE BEEN IN KIND OF A FUNK LATELY.
THE BREAK-UP... TEACHING UNDER-GRADS... PROF. JONES DRIVING ME CRAZY...
JORGE CHAM © 2009
IT'S LIKE I DON'T EVEN KNOW WHY I'M DOING THIS ANYMORE!
YOU MEAN YOU KNEW BEFORE?
FUNKS ARE TEMPORARY, RIGHT?
WHAT A YEAR THIS HAS BEEN!
SO FULL OF CHANGES AND CHALLENGES...
JORGE CHAM © 2008
IT'S LIKE THE WHOLE WORLD IS NOW INHALING, WAITING FOR AN UNCERTAIN FUTURE WITH TREPIDATION AND HOPE.
I MIGHT LEARN LaTeX THIS YEAR.
SOME GRAD STUDENTS EXCEPTED.

JORGE CHAM © 2009
send
Your Holidays grace period is now officially over.
What's new?
HEY, I JUST GOT A NOTICE SAYING MY GREEN CARD APPLI-CATION PASSED THE FIRST STAGE...
THAT'S GREAT!
I'M SO HAPPY FOR YOU! IMAGINE FINALLY HAVING A GREEN CARD..!
JORGE CHAM © 2009
NO MORE VISA REQUIREMENTS OR WAITING IN LINE...
NO MORE RESTRICTIONS ON WHERE YOU CAN WORK...
WE SHOULD CELEBRATE!
WE SHOULD GET MARRIED.
EXCUSE ME?

LOOK, I KNOW YOU'RE CATEGORICALLY OPPOSED TO THE IDEA OF MARRIAGE...
OF COURSE!
MARRIAGE IS AN OPPRESSIVE INSTITUTION CONSTRUED BY A PATRIARCHAL SOCIETY TO PROMOTE ANTIQUATED AND DISCRIMINATORY GENDER ROLES!
JORGE CHAM © 2009
RIGHT. BUT IF WE GET MARRIED NOW, BEFORE THE NEXT STEP IN MY APPLICATION, THE LAW SAYS YOU GET A GREEN CARD TOO.
YOU'D BE USING MARRIAGE AS A TOOL FOR SUBVERSION!
THIS HAS TO BE THE STRANGEST PROPOSAL EVER.
THE GREEN CARD IS NOT THE ONLY REASON I WANT TO MARRY YOU, TAJEL.
THE TRUTH IS, IF TWO PEOPLE LOVE EACH OTHER, THEY SHOULDN'T HAVE TO GET MARRIED TO PROVE IT...
JORGE CHAM © 2009
BUT I LOVE YOU, TAJEL, AND I WOULD DO ANYTHING THAT HELPS KEEP US TOGETHER.
EVEN IF LOVE IS JUST A CONTEXTUALLY CONTINGENT PSYCHO-SOCIAL CONSTRUCT?
ESPECIALLY SO.

SO, WHAT DID YOU WANT TO TELL ME?
I'LL WAIT UNTIL YOU PUT YOUR DRINK DOWN.
OK.
I'M GETTING MARRIED.
JORGE CHAM © 2009
PFFTT!!
WHAT??
TAJEL, YOU CAN'T MARRY PATRICK!
HE'S A PROFESSOR! YOU'RE STILL IN GRAD SCHOOL! THAT HAS TO BE AGAINST SCHOOL POLICY...
JORGE CHAM © 2009
AND WHAT ABOUT YOUR THESIS? SHOULDN'T YOU BE FOCUSING ON THAT?
YOU'RE TAKING SUCH A HUGE STEP!
ARE YOU SAYING WE SHOULD GET MY ADVISOR'S PERMISSION FIRST?
WHY STOP NOW?

PROF. RIVERA, THIS IS AWKWARD, BUT I THOUGHT YOU SHOULD KNOW THAT-
WAIT, WAIT.
IS THIS SOMETHING PERSONAL? BECAUSE IF IT IS, I'D RATHER YOU DIDN'T TELL ME.
JORGE CHAM © 2009
AS A PROFESSOR, IT MAKES MY JOB A LOT EASIER IF I DON'T THINK OF YOU AS HAVING A LIFE OUTSIDE OF RESEARCH.
OTHERWISE, YOU'RE LIKE THIS... THIS...
REAL PERSON?
ONE OF THOSE, YEAH.

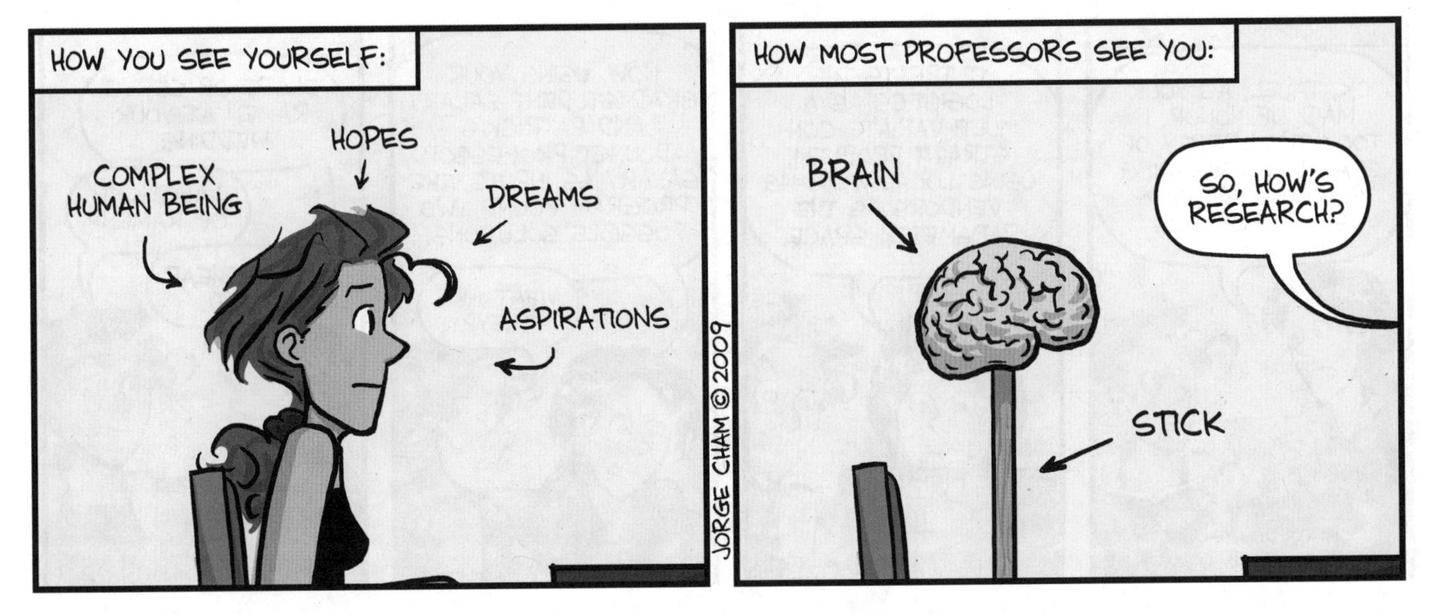
HOW YOU SEE YOURSELF:
HOPES
COMPLEX HUMAN BEING
DREAMS
ASPIRATIONS
JORGE CHAM © 2009
HOW MOST PROFESSORS SEE YOU:
BRAIN
SO, HOW'S RESEARCH?
STICK

SO, YOU'RE GETTING MARRIED, THAT'S... GOOD. WHO'S THE LUCKY INDIVIDUAL?
UH...
ACTUALLY, IT'S PROF. KHUMALO.
PROF. KHUMALO? IN OUR DEPARTMENT? HMMMM...
THIS IS A VERY SERIOUS MATTER, TAJEL. I'LL HAVE TO CONSULT WITH THE DEPARTMENT CHAIR, PROF. STEIN, ABOUT THIS.
YES, OF C-
JORGE CHAM © 2009
WAIT, AREN'T YOU MARRIED TO PROF. STEIN?
WE'RE AN INCESTUOUS DEPARTMENT. IT SHOULDN'T BE A PROBLEM.
OK, TAJEL, AS YOUR MAID OF HONOR, I TOOK THE LIBERTY OF STARTING A WEDDING PLANNING SPREAD-SHEET FOR YOU.
IT TREATS THE LOGISTICS AS A MULTI-VARIATE CON-STRAINT PROBLEM, USING LOCAL WEDDING VENDORS AS THE PARAMETER SPACE.
JORGE CHAM © 2009
NOW, USING YOUR GRAD STUDENT SALARY AND PATRICK'S ADJUNCT PROFESSOR SALARY AS INPUTS, THE PROGRAM FOUND TWO POSSIBLE SOLUTIONS.
WHAT ARE THEY?
ELOPE OR SERVE RAMEN AT YOUR WEDDING.
WHAT KIND OF RAMEN?
THE CHEAP KIND.

THE ECONOMIC CRISIS TAKES ITS TOLL

TAJEL, WE TRIED TO MAKE YOUR WEDDING AS SOCIALLY RESPONSIBLE AS POSSIBLE.
THE GUESTBOOK THE GUESTS ARE SIGNING IS ACTUALLY A PETITION FOR AFFORDABLE GRAD HOUSING...
INSTEAD OF A REGISTRY, WE'RE HAVING PEOPLE DONATE TO CHARITY...
??
Grad Students Without Borders
THE OFFICIANT IS ACTUALLY A HOMELESS MAN WE GOT LICENSED BY THE STATE YESTERDAY.
IN FACT, THE WHOLE WEDDING IS DOUBLING AS A STAGED PROTEST FOR UNIVERSITY DIVESTMENT.
IVEST
NOW
TO TOP IT OFF, ALL THE FOOD IS LOCAL, FAIR TRADE, ORGANIC, AND, OF COURSE...
JORGE CHAM © 2009
...SOY-BASED VEGAN.
PFFT!

I'M A LITTLE NERVOUS ABOUT THEM MEETING, PATRICK.
NAH...
I'M SURE THEY'LL GET ALONG!
WHAT IF THEY DON'T LIKE EACH OTHER??
ARE YOU KIDDING? YOUR PARENTS ARE GREAT! I'M SURE MY PARENTS WILL LOVE THEM!
I WAS TALKING ABOUT MY PROFESSOR.
YOU INVITED HIM?
MOM, DAD, THIS IS PROF. RIVERA, MY ADVISOR.
HELLO.
HELLO! HOW ARE YOU?
I FEEL LIKE I ALREADY KNOW YOU, PROFESSOR. TAJEL TALKS ABOUT YOU ALL THE TIME.
ALL GOOD THINGS, I HOPE?
JORGE CHAM © 2009
UH...
OF COURSE!
SO, WHICH ONE OF US IS GIVING YOU AWAY?

ARE YOU READY?
YEAH.
CECILIA... ARE YOU GOING TO BE ALLRIGHT?
WELL, SOME OF THAT VEGAN FOOD IS MAKING MY STOMACH QUEAZY.
I MEANT, IN GENERAL...
I KNOW YOU'VE BEEN KIND OF BUMMED LATELY, AND NOW I'M GOING TO BE MOVING OUT.
I WON'T BE THERE AS YOUR ROOMATE ANYMORE...
I'LL BE FINE, TAJEL, DON'T WORRY.
MAYBE I JUST NEED TO DO SOMETHING DRAMATIC LIKE YOU AND GET MARRIED OR SOMETHING!
JORGE CHAM © 2009
OR YOU COULD GRADUATE.
WHAT? WHOA! I SAID DRAMATIC, NOT CRAZY!

PATRICK...
SOMETIMES IT'S EASY TO GET CAUGHT UP IN THE HARDSHIPS AND FRUSTRATIONS OF GRAD SCHOOL...
...AND THINK THAT MAYBE WHAT WE'VE DONE HASN'T BEEN WORTH IT.
BUT THEN I THINK ABOUT ALL THE PEOPLE I'VE MET ALONG THE WAY.
FRIENDS THAT HAVE STOOD BY ME AND MADE IT ALL BEARABLE.
ESPECIALLY YOU, PATRICK...
...AND I KNOW IT'S WORTH MORE THAN ANY DIPLOMA I WILL EVER RECEIVE.
JORGE CHAM © 2009
I'M GLAD I CAME TO GRAD SCHOOL. OTHERWISE I WOULDN'T HAVE FOUND YOU.

HERE ARE MY VOWS TO YOU, TAJEL...
I PROMISE TO BE WITH YOU, IN TENURE OR UNEMPLOYMENT (OR WHATEVER YOU CALL BEING AN ADJUNCT).
FOR BETTER, WORSE, OR INCONCLUSIVE.
IN AGREEMENT OR DISAGREEMENT OVER ANTHROPOLOGICAL METHODOLOGY...
IN SICKNESS OR IN CASE WE EVER GET HEALTHCARE...
FOR THE REST OF MY ACADEMIC LIFE.*
*(FOOTNOTE: PROFESSORS NEVER RETIRE)
are we done yet?
F. BOAS
S
JORGE CHAM © 2009
MAYBE IT IS TIME I FINALLY GRADUATED.

PHD Tales from the Road Comics

JORGE CHAM ©2007

PHD TALES FROM THE ROAD PRESENTS:
IT'S BEAUTIFUL ALL THE WAY DOWN
CONVERSATIONS WITH ASTROPHYSICISTS
PART 1
PHD MAKES ITS FIRST TRANSATLANTIC TRIP FOR A TALK AT THE CANARY ISLANDS' ASTROPHYSICS INSTITUTE
SPAIN
AFRICA
EVENT ORGANIZER NOELIA, AN ARGENTINE, WAS SURPRISED I ACCEPTED THE INVITATION:
I THOUGHT YOU WERE MORE FAMOUS THAN THAT.
I'M EASY.*
LONG HAIRDO
* TRANSLATED FROM SPANISH
AMID THE MARS-LIKE LANDSCAPE ON TOP OF "EL TEIDE", TENERIFE'S MAIN VOLCANO, I GET A TOUR OF THE TELESCOPE FACILITIES.
SO WHERE ARE ALL THE STARS?
THAT'S THE LIQUID NITROGEN NOZZLE.
ALSO, IT'S THE MIDDLE OF THE DAY.
IN ACTUALITY, TIME ON THE BIG TELESCOPES IS VERY PRECIOUS (AND EXPENSIVE). YOU ONLY GET A COUPLE OF WEEKS DURING YOUR ENTIRE PH.D., SO YOU BETTER MAKE THEM COUNT!
AT A TYPICAL SESSION, YOU SPEND NIGHT AFTER NIGHT IN ISOLATION, NOT WASTING ONE MINUTE, CHECKING ON THE EQUIPMENT AS PHOTONS FROM STARS BILLIONS OF MILES AWAY AND MILLIONS OF YEARS OLD IMPINGE ON YOUR CALIBRATED CCD SENSORS, HOPING THEY CARRY DATA GOOD ENOUGH FOR A THESIS.
JORGE CHAM © 2007
ZZZZ

MY TOURGUIDE CONRADO DESCRBES A FRIEND'S THESIS, WHICH PROPOSED A NEW METHOD FOR FINDING STARS THAT HAVE PLANETS ORBITING AROUND THEM.
OF COURSE, HE HAD TO SHOW IT WORKED.
TALK ABOUT FINDING A THESIS IN A HAY STACK! LUCKILY, IT ONLY TOOK 5 YEARS.
PLANET FOUND!
SOB!
STILL, I'M SURE IT'S ALL WORTH IT.
SO WHAT DO YOU DO WITH AN ASTROPHYSICS DEGREE?
BEATS ME, I'M GOING INTO BUSINESS CONSULTING.
OF COURSE, NOT ALL ASTRONOMERS WORK WITH TELESCOPES. SOME ONLY DO COMPUTER SIMULATIONS, LIKE JORGE (NICE NAME!), A NATIVE CANARIAN AND COMIC BOOK AFICIONADO
WE STARE AT THE COMPUTER SO LONG, WE START TO SEE STARS ANYWAY.
HE INVITES ME TO HIS BIRTHDAY PARTY, WHICH LASTS OVER 8 HOURS (CANARIANS TAKE THEIR PARTYING SERIOUSLY).
OUR KING IS USELESS
BUT WE LOVE HIM ANYWAY
MIGUEL 1
MIGUEL 2
RECENTLY AT PRINCETON, ANOTHER GROUP OF ASTROPHYSICISTS TAKE ME OUT TO DINNER (AND ICE CREAM OF COURSE).
THEY DESCRIBE TO ME WHAT THEY DO ON LONG FLIGHTS WHEN ASKED THE DREADED:
SO, WHAT DO YOU DO?
UH...
IF YOU FEEL LIKE TALKING, ANSWER:
I'M AN ASTRONOMER.
WOW! TELL ME MORE!
TO KILL THE CONVERSATION:
I'M A PHYSICIST.
ZZZZZ!

RISING ASTROPHYSICS STAR (NO PUN INTENDED) KATIE DESCRIBES HER RESEARCH: MINI BLACK HOLES, WHICH HAVE THE MASS OF A MOUNTAIN IN THE SIZE OF A PEA.
APPARENTLY, THESE MINI BLACK HOLES ARE ZOOMING ALL AROUND US, AND COULD ANNIHILATE YOU INSTANTLY.
I'M NOT WORRIED THOUGH.
OF COURSE, SHE'S NEVER SEEN ONE. IT'S ALL THEORETICAL. I PRESS THEM ON THIS POINT.
SO MUCH OF WHAT ASTROPHYSICISTS CLAIM, NOBODY'S EVER SEEN!
WE CAN'T SEE IT, BUT WE **KNOW** IT'S THERE.
FOR EXAMPLE, TO EXPLAIN THE GRAVITATIONAL TRAJECTORIES OF CERTAIN GALAXIES, THEY INVENTED "DARK MATTER". THE UNIVERSE IS EXPANDING FASTER THAN PREDICTED? BLAME IT ON "DARK ENERGY".
SO, IF YOU HAVE NO CLUE ABOUT SOMETHING...
WE PUT "DARK" IN FRONT OF IT. IT'S EASIER TO GET FUNDING.
I HAVE A DARK THESIS.
FROM OBSERVATIONS OF WHOLE GALAXIES AND NEBULAE, THEORIES ARE BUILT ABOUT THE ORIGIN AND BUILDING BLOCKS OF OUR UNIVERSE.
IS THERE A GRAND THEORY OF EVERYTHING? SOME PHYSICISTS SAY "WHY BOTHER?", SUBSCRIBING TO THE ANTHROPIC PRINCIPLE:
THINGS (QUARKS, LEPTONS) ARE THE WAY THEY ARE SIMPLY BECAUSE IF THEY WEREN'T, WE WOULDN'T BE HERE TO ASK THIS QUESTION.
WHY ME?
WHY NOT?
THE BIG BANG? WE KNOW IT HAPPENED BECAUSE OF ONE MEASUREMENT OF THE UNIVERSE'S BACK-GROUND NOISE.
Intensity, 10⁻⁴ ergs / cm² sr sec cm⁻¹
Waves / centimeter
THAT'S IT?
KATIE ADAMANTLY REFUSES TO ACCEPT THIS:
IN OTHER WORDS, THERE ISN'T A GRAND EQUATION AT THE HEART OF EVERYTHING, SO WE SHOULD STOP LOOKING.
SO FAR, ALL OF REALITY SEEMS TO BE DESCRIBED BY EXQUISITE, ELEGANT MATHEMATICAL EQUATIONS.
WE CAN'T GIVE UP NOW. IT'S GOTTA BE BEAUTIFUL ALL THE WAY DOWN.

PHD TALES FROM THE ROAD
"FORREST GUMP GOES TO GERMANY"
-PART 1
JORGE CHAM © 2008
RECENTLY, I WAS INVITED TO SPEAK AT A DEPARTMENT RETREAT IN TULANE UNIVERSITY.
CAN WE GET A DISCOUNT ON YOUR SPEAKING FEE?
ACTUALLY, THE RETREAT WAS IN MISSISSIPPI, 1.5 HRS AWAY FROM THE AIRPORT. MY RIDE ON THIS LONG TRIP WAS TODD FELTON, A GRAD STUDENT IN BIOMEDICAL SCIENCES AND A TRUE SON OF THE BAYOU.
HOWDY, DR. CHAM!
PHD GUY
UNLIKE MOST OF US WHO WENT TO GRAD SCHOOL STRAIGHT OUT OF COLLEGE, TODD FOLLOWED A LESS DIRECT PATH...
"I WAS KIND OF A REBEL. DROPPED OUT OF COLLEGE A FEW TIMES...
"BOUNCED AROUND, ENDED UP AS AN EMT (EMERGENCY MEDICAL TECHNICIAN) FOR 10 YEARS..."
"FINALLY, MY WIFE SAID TO ME:
WHAT ARE YOU DOING WITH YOUR LIFE?
FOR INSPIRATION, HE CONSULTED HIS CHILDHOOD HEROES:
MR. SPOCK
JACQUES COUSTEAU
GO BACK TO SCHOOL.
YESSIR.
SEVERAL YEARS IN, HE'S NOW EVEN HOBNOBBING WITH NOBEL LAUREATES!
RECENTLY, HE WON A PRESTIGIOUS INVITATION TO THE LINDAU MEETING, A GET-TOGETHER WHERE ONLY NOBEL WINNERS AND A FEW STUDENTS ARE INVITED.
HUH. SMALLER THAN I THOUGHT.
BECAUSE OF HIS BAYOU ROOTS AND SOUTHERN DRAWL, HIS LABMATES JOKINGLY CALLED IT, "FORREST GUMP GOES TO GERMANY"
SCIENCE IS AS SCIENCE DOES.

STILL, DON'T BE FOOLED... HIS DESCRIPTION OF HIS LAB'S RESEARCH LEAVES MY HEAD SPINNING:
BASICALLY, WE CREATE BIOLOGICAL SENSORS FOR DETECTING URANIUM IN CONTAMINATED GROUND WATER.
1
FIRST, WE BOND A SAMPLE ION OF UO_2^{2+} TO A PROTEIN VIA A DICARBOXYLIC MOLECULE WE CREATE.
URANIUM
PROTEIN
2
WE INJECT THAT INTO A MOUSE AND WAIT FOR ITS IMMUNE SYSTEM TO GENERATE ANTI-BODIES AGAINST THIS FOREIGN COMPOUND.
B-CELL
CANCER CELL
3
THEN WE TAKE CELLS FROM ITS SPLEEN AND FUSE THEM WITH CANCER CELLS USING ANTI-FREEZE.
CANCER CELLS?? WHERE DO YOU GET CANCER CELLS!?
WE BUY 'EM. THERE'S A CATALOG FOR 'EM.
THE ANTI-FREEZE SOFTENS THE CELL MEMBRANES AND FUSES THEM TO CREATE MUTANT ANTI-BODY-PRODUCING CANCER CELLS.
4
BECAUSE THE CELLS ARE CANCEROUS, THEY REPLICATE INDEFINITELY, GIVING YOU AN ENDLESS SOURCE OF THE RIGHT ANTI-BODY.
BY LABELLING THE ANTI-BODY MOLECULES AND EXPOSING THEM TO THE GROUND WATER, WE CAN TELL HOW MUCH URANIUM THERE IS.
U!
5
THE CELLS WILL KEEP IN THE FREEZER UNTIL YOU NEED MORE ANTI-BODIES MADE.
HOLY S#&%! SO YOU CREATED A LIVING ORGANISM ENGINEERED TO PRODUCE A SPECIFIC MOLECULE FOR AN INTENDED USE??
YEAH, YOU LEARN THAT YOUR FIRST YEAR.
I AM BLOWN AWAY BY THIS! WHEN DID HUMANS LEARN TO CONTROL AND MANIPULATE NATURE LIKE THAT? SUCH MASTERY OF LIFE ITSELF!
NATURE, OF COURSE, BEGS TO DIFFER...
NEXT: TULANE AND KATRINA!

PHD TALES FROM THE ROAD
"FORREST GUMP GOES TO GERMANY"
- PART 2
TULANE IS IN NEW ORLEANS, AND AS WE DRIVE TO THE RETREAT SITE, I GET A TOUR OF THE AREAS DEVASTATED BY KATRINA AND THE STORM SURGE, WHICH ACTED LIKE A TSUNAMI.
THIS WHOLE AREA WAS UNDER WATER.
JEFFERSON PARISH
JORGE CHAM © 2008
WHEN THE ORDER TO EVACUATE CAME, TODD WAS IN WEEK 10 OF A 12 WEEK EXPERIMENT.
BUT I'M IN WEEK 10 OF A 12 WEEK EXPERIMENT!
LEAVE, YOU DUMBASS.
(WIFE)
LIKE HIS WIFE, WHO STAYED FOR 3 DAYS IN THE LOCAL HOSPITAL, HAVING TO DIP CAST DRESSINGS IN 3FT. OF FLOOD WATER.
HE SAYS A LOT OF BAD CAME OUT IN PEOPLE, BUT ALSO A LOT OF GOOD.
IN AN EVEN MORE AMAZING DISPLAY OF JOB DEDICATION, JANE, THEIR LAB TECHNICIAN, STAYED BEHIND FOR 5 DAYS IN THE LAB, WITH NO POWER, TO LOOK AFTER THE ANIMALS AND EQUIPMENT.
I HAVE GIRL-SCOUT TRAINING.
FINALLY, THEY HAD TO PULL HER OUT BY HELICOPTER.
WAIT! THE NITROGEN TANKS!
EVENTUALLY, TODD WENT HOME AND RODE OUT THE STORM AND THE CHAOS, FENDING OFF LOOTERS...

TODD ALSO VOLUNTEERED HIS EMT TRAINING, THOUGH FINDING ANYTHING IN THE RAVAGED GULF PORT AREA WAS A MESS.
EMERGENCY CALL. MAKE A LEFT AT THE WENDY'S.
WHAT WENDY'S??
SURVIVORS WOULD LATER SWAP HARROWING STORIES AND COMPARE DAMAGE TO THEIR HOMES:
MIRACULOUSLY SPARED.
"GONE"
"SLAB GONE"
AFTER THE STORM, MANY STUDENTS AND FACULTY FOUND REFUGE IN OTHER UNIVERSITIES, WHO KINDLY OPENED THEIR DOORS.
GOT ROOM FOR MY LAB EQUIPMENT TOO?
NOT EVERYONE WAS ASKED TO COME BACK, THOUGH.
AT THE RETREAT'S BONFIRE, I GET THE SKINNY ON THE UNIVERSITY'S
RENEWAL PLAN!
CITING "ECONOMIC DISTRESS", THE SCHOOL ELIMINATED MANY TENURED FACULTY POSITIONS, EVEN WHOLE DEPARTMENTS.
HUMANITIES, ARTS, ENGINEERING...
ENGINEERING!? GONE!?
SLAB GONE!
TENURED PROFESSORS! FIRED! IMAGINE THE OUTRAGE! CRITICS SAY THE SCHOOL IS USING KATRINA AS AN EXCUSE TO "CLEAN HOUSE" AND GET RID OF PROFESSORS AND RESEARCH PROGRAMS WITH SUB-PAR PERFORMANCE.
BASICALLY, ANYONE WHO COULDN'T GET NIH (NATL. INST. OF HEALTH) GRANTS WAS BOOTED.
MY PROF. HAD TO FIND A CORPORATE RESEARCH JOB.
HONESTLY, I THINK HE'S HAPPIER.
STILL, LIFE (AND SLOW RECONSTRUCTION) GOES ON IN THE GULF REGION.
TODD SAYS MANY SURVIVORS STILL SUFFER FROM POST TRAUMATIC STRESS DISORDER, EVEN AS MANY OTHERS START TO GROW COMPLACENT.
BEACH FRONT PROPERTY! SWEET!
AS HE DROPS ME OFF AT THE AIRPORT, TODD THANKS ME FOR DRAWING PHD COMICS.
YOU HELP GRAD STUDENTS NOT QUIT.
UH...

PHD TALES FROM THE ROAD PRESENTS
DON'T LICK THE SPOON
JORGE CHAM © 2008
A SHORT TOUR OF TWO CHEMISTRY LABS
ON A RECENT TRIP TO WASHINGTON UNIVERSITY (AT ST. LOUIS), I GET A TOUR OF THE CHEMISTRY LABS, WHERE THERE'S ALWAYS SOMETHING SIMMERING ON A HOT PLATE:
CHEMISTRY IS LIKE COOKING!
BUT DON'T LICK THE SPOON.
ONE OF THE STUDENTS, JEREMY, HAS A DIFFERENT ANALOGY:
HIS CURRENT EXPERIMENT INVOLVES RUNNING A SUBSTANCE THROUGH A FILTER AND WATCHING IT DRIP FOR HOURS, CHANGING TEST TUBES EVERY TWO MINUTES.
IT'S LIKE CHINESE WATER TORTURE!
NOT ON A TYPICAL KITCHEN, HOWEVER, ARE THE PRESSURIZED GLOVE BOXES, WHICH HOLD CHEMICALS THAT WOULD EXPLODE ON CONTACT WITH AIR.
IS THAT DUCT TAPE?
WE USE IT TO PATCH LEAKS
CHEMISTS USE NUCLEAR MAGNETIC RESONANCE (NMR) TO DETERMINE THE STRUCTURE OF THE COMPOUNDS THEY CREATE. A TYPICAL NMR PLOT LOOKS LIKE THIS:
PPM
THOUGH THEY LOOK LIKE RANDOM PEAKS TO ME, A TRAINED CHEMIST CAN TELL WHAT MOLECULE IT REPRESENTS:
OBVIOUSLY, THAT'S A TRIPLE BOND AROMATIC CH-OH GROUP
OBVIOUSLY.

AT THE UNIVERSITY OF LOUISVILLE, UNDERGRAD JESSE EXPANDS ON THE COOKING ANALOGY:
CHEMISTRY IS LIKE A GIANT COOKBOOK OF RECIPES FOR KNOWN REACTIONS...
The Joy of Chemistry
"BUT THERE IS STILL A LOT WE DON'T KNOW. THE RECIPES MAY TELL YOU WHAT HAPPENS WHEN YOU MIX TWO PARTICULAR THINGS TOGETHER, BUT THEY DON'T TELL YOU WHY IT HAPPENS."
JESSE IS ALSO PRESIDENT OF THE "SOCIETY OF UNDERGRADUATE CHEMISTRY STUDENTS."
S.U.C.S.?
YES, IT DOES.
ALSO AT WASH. U...
I MEET KARTHIK, WHOSE PROFES-SOR TOLD HIM TO "CLEAN UP" BEFORE GOING TO INTERVIEWS:
BEFORE
AFTER
I WOULDN'T HIRE YOU.
I STILL CAN'T GET A JOB!
...AND I MEET DIANA, WHOSE NAPPING SKILLS ARE FAMOUS IN HER DEPARTMENT. SHE ACTUALLY BOUGHT A COT THAT SHE STORES IN A SECRET ROOM IN HER BUILDING.
ZZZ
ZZZ
ZZZ

PHD Tales from The Road Presents:
Gee Whiz!
Or "We love Marx!"
JORGE CHAM © 2008
My next stop on the speaking tour: Bowling Green, Ohio! Home of:
The National Tractor Pulling Championships!
The Department of Popular Culture at Bowling Green University!
I sit down to talk with several of these Pop Culture Scholars, including:
Amanda, who is still studying the Dave Matthews Band phenomenon (see the comic from 7/4/06)...
yep, still in Grad School.
...and Dan, who studies how amateur musicians are portrayed in movies.
they're used as a tool to marginalize and assign credibility in art
What does it all mean? Dan chuckles:
don't you know? conclusions are considered "imperialistic" in the Humanities!
there are many truths
and many theses?
Other stuff they don't like:
Hegemony
the assumption of superiority by a dominant culture.
Stuff they do like:
We love Marx!
Karl
Groucho
Richard

Having to teach Microsoft Word's spell-checker new words invented by their field:

Heteronormatism

Problematizing

Homosocial

Othering

why don't you just say "creates problem"?

then you can't take credit for it.

Can you imagine the conversation they would have?

Pop Quiz!

By being featured in this comic, does the Department *itself* enter Pop Culture!? Discuss.

Dan acknowledges it's sometimes hard to get people to take their work seriously.

"When people think of us, they often think of the comic book guy from The Simpsons."

The Humanities (and especially us) are often accused of being a "Gee Whiz" field that's good for nothing.

(and believe me, nobody stresses out about being relevant more than us)

But social and cultural forces are real things that affect people's well-being and how they fare in society.

Hopefully, by talking about it and teaching students, we can all learn to recognize these invisible Power Structures that oppress in unconscious ways.

It's not going to immediately help poor families, for example, but it may help future generations pull themselves out of their situations.

MY TRAVELS TAKE ME TO... WISCONSIN!
PHD TALES FROM THE ROAD PRESENTS "THE GENERATION GAP"
JORGE CHAM © 2008
I GIVE A TALK FOR THE MEDICAL COLLEGE OF WISCONSIN, WHERE I MEET RICHARD, WHO SAYS HE WANTS TO JOIN THE FBI AFTER HE GRADUATES WITH A PH.D. IN BIOMEDICAL SCIENCES.
TO DO FORENSIC RESEARCH?
NAH, I'M SICK OF LAB WORK.
I WANT TO BE A FIELD AGENT AND SHOOT PEOPLE!
ANOTHER GRAD STUDENT, DAN, ALSO REVEALS HIS DOUBTS ABOUT A RESEARCH CAREER. HIS REAL PASSION IS TO BE A COUNSELOR FOR CHRISTIAN CAMPS.
THERE HAS TO BE A PURPOSE TO LIFE.
IT CAN'T JUST BE ABOUT EATING AND REPRODUCING.
"THAT SOUNDS PRETTY GOOD TO ME!" SAYS DR. GRIFFITH, THE DEAN OF THE SCHOOL. HE SAYS HIS GENERATION HAD FEWER CAREER OPTIONS.
FOR ME, IT WAS GO TO GRAD SCHOOL OR GO TO VIETNAM.
(DURING THE WAR, ATTENDING A UNIVERSITY DEFERRED YOU FROM THE DRAFT)
WHEN THE DRAFT SWITCHED TO A LOTTERY, JOHN, WHO'S BACK IN GRAD SCHOOL AFTER YEARS IN INDUSTRY, WASN'T SO LUCKY AND JOINED THE ARMY.
HEY, I USED TO DRAW CARTOONS FOR MY COLLEGE PAPER TOO!
COOL!
...BUT THEN I WENT TO VIETNAM AND NOTHING SEEMED FUNNY ANYMORE.
HE TELLS ME HARROWING STORIES OF FLYING HELICOPTERS DURING STRESSFUL MILITARY OPERATIONS.
"EVERYTHING IS PLANNED TO A 'T'",
"UNTIL SOMETHING GOES WRONG."
#@$%!!
THAT SAME WEEK, AT THE UNIVERSITY OF WISCONSIN-MADISON, I'M GREETED BY A LARGE CROWD AND, OF COURSE...
WISCONSIN CHEESE!!
HMM, NOT AS GOOD AS CALIFORNIA CHEESE.
OK, GET OUT.
GRAD STUDENT SARAH DESCRIBES HER DEVELOPMENTAL PSYCHOLOGY RESEARCH:
I EXPERIMENT ON BABIES.
THEY DO IT FOR THE FREE MILK.
WHOOPS, IT'S NAP TIME!
ZZZ...

COLLISIONS
VISITING CERN
PART 1
A PILED HIGHER AND DEEPER "TALES FROM THE ROAD"
ON A RECENT TRIP TO GENEVA, I GOT A TOUR OF CERN (THE EUROPEAN ORGANIZATION FOR NUCLEAR RESEARCH), HOME OF THE LARGE HADRON COLLIDER (LHC), THE WORLD'S LARGEST PARTICLE ACCELERATOR.
MY TOUR GUIDE: BENOIT, A PH.D. STUDENT FROM EPFL.
UH, SHOULD I BE WEARING A RADIATION BADGE TOO?
NAH.
JORGE CHAM © 20
IMAGINE TWO BEAMS OF PARTICLES TRAVELING AT 0.999 THE SPEED OF LIGHT...
EACH MADE OF PROTONS BUNCHED TOGETHER CARRYING THE EQUIVALENT ENERGY OF AN AIRCRAFT CARRIER AT 60 km/h AND SQUEEZED INTO AN AREA THE SIZE OF YOUR PINKY FINGER.
THE TWO BEAMS CIRCLE EACH OTHER AROUND A 27 km UNDERGROUND TUNNEL NEAR THE SWISS ALPS UNTIL...
GENEVA
...AN OPERATOR HITS A SWITCH AND THEY COLLIDE!
WHAT HAPPENS NEXT??
UH, WHO KNOWS?

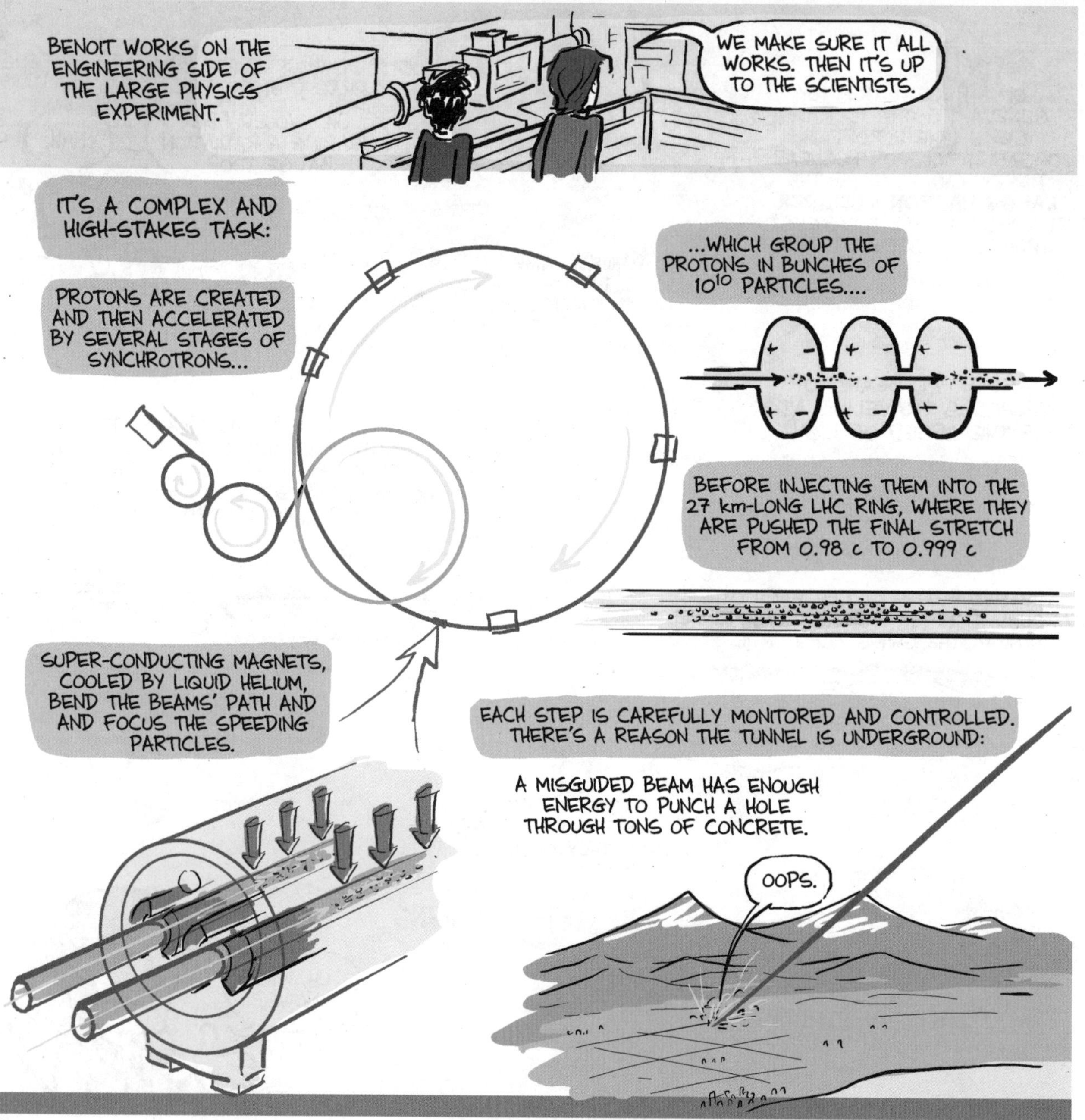
BENOIT WORKS ON THE ENGINEERING SIDE OF THE LARGE PHYSICS EXPERIMENT.
WE MAKE SURE IT ALL WORKS. THEN IT'S UP TO THE SCIENTISTS.
IT'S A COMPLEX AND HIGH-STAKES TASK:
PROTONS ARE CREATED AND THEN ACCELERATED BY SEVERAL STAGES OF SYNCHROTRONS...
...WHICH GROUP THE PROTONS IN BUNCHES OF 10^{10} PARTICLES....
BEFORE INJECTING THEM INTO THE 27 km-LONG LHC RING, WHERE THEY ARE PUSHED THE FINAL STRETCH FROM 0.98 c TO 0.999 c
SUPER-CONDUCTING MAGNETS, COOLED BY LIQUID HELIUM, BEND THE BEAMS' PATH AND AND FOCUS THE SPEEDING PARTICLES.
EACH STEP IS CAREFULLY MONITORED AND CONTROLLED. THERE'S A REASON THE TUNNEL IS UNDERGROUND:
A MISGUIDED BEAM HAS ENOUGH ENERGY TO PUNCH A HOLE THROUGH TONS OF CONCRETE.
OOPS.

COLLISIONS
PART 2
PHD TALES FROM THE ROAD
WE CROSS THE BORDER INTO FRANCE FOR A VISIT TO THE ACCELERATOR CONTROL ROOM...
DID YOU BRING YOUR PASSPORT?
OUI.
IT'S SURPRISINGLY RELAXED.
WE'RE ON DOWN TIME.
WHEN IT'S GO TIME, IT'S A TENSE 8 MINUTES AS THE BEAMS RAMP UP AND MAKE THEIR WAY THROUGH THE SYNCHROTRONS. NOTHING CAN GO WRONG!
DON'T BLOW UP... DON'T BLOW UP...
IF SOMETHING DOES GO WRONG, IT'S NOT THE PHYSICAL DAMAGE THAT WORRIES THEM
WE GOT SPARES
CAN I TAKE ONE HOME?
THE REAL COST IS IN RESETTING THE EXPERIMENT. IT CAN TAKE MONTHS TO PREP THE MAGNETS AGAIN.
IT BROKE AGAIN.
WOO HOO!
I ASK BENOIT HOW HE GOT INTO PARTICLE PHYSICS.
IT WAS KIND OF A RANDOM COLLISION, ACTUALLY...
MY GIRLFRIEND MOVED TO GENEVA AND I NEEDED A JOB.
THE THINGS WE DO FOR LOVE...
PHYSICS!
STILL, I CAN TELL HE FINDS IT EXCITING:
THE SIZE AND COMPLEXITY OF THIS PROJECT IS INCREDIBLE.
THIS IS LIKE DISNEYLAND!
ON THE WAY OUT, HE POINTS OUT WHERE ALL THE REALLY IMPORTANT DECISIONS GET MADE AROUND HERE:
THE CAFETERIA?
OVER COFFEE.

IS IT WORTH THE BILLIONS OF EUROS THIS PROJECT COSTS?
MAYBE IT'S ALL A BIG WASTE OF RESOURCES...
BUT AT THE VERY LEAST IT HAS LED TO MANY INNOVATIONS IN TECHNOLOGY.
COMPUTING
WWW.
MEDICAL IMAGING
JORGE CHAM © 2008
IN ANY CASE, IT'S A QUESTION WE HAVE TO ASK OURSELVES AS HUMANS: WHAT ARE WE MADE OF?
SCIENCE DELIVERY!
NO SOLICITORS
WE'RE KNOCKING ON THE DOOR OF REALITY...
WHO KNOWS WHAT'S ON THE OTHER SIDE?
I ASK BENOIT WHY HE VOLUNTEERED TO SHOW ME AROUND ALL AFTERNOON, EVEN THOUGH HE'D NEVER HEARD OF ME OR PHD COMICS.
WELL, IT'S INTERESTING TO WORK ON THIS STUFF...
BUT IT'S ALSO INTERESTING TO SHARE IT.
COLLISIONS
PHD TALES FROM THE ROAD
PART 3
LATER, A COUPLE MORE PEOPLE AGREE TO HANG OUT AND TALK TO ME ABOUT THEIR WORK.
TRUST ME, I KNOW ALL THE GOOD BARS.
WE HAD NO IDEA WHAT YOU'D LOOK LIKE.
POSTDOC TERESA, ONE OF THE 9% OF FEMALE PHYSICISTS AT CERN, EXPLAINS WHAT THE COLLIDER IS:
IT'S JUST A TOOL.
LIKE A GIANT MICROSCOPE.
ON A REGULAR MICROSCOPE, YOU STUDY A SAMPLE BY HITTING IT WITH PHOTONS AND THEN OBSERVING WHAT HAPPENS TO THOSE PHOTONS.
WE'RE GONNA NEED A BIGGER LENS.
HERE, WHAT YOU ARE TRYING TO OBSERVE IS SO SMALL, YOU RUN INTO THE HEISENBERG PRINCIPLE, BUT THE CONCEPT IS THE SAME:
YOU HIT THINGS TOGETHER AND SEE WHAT HAPPENS.

THERE ARE SEVERAL EXPERIMENTS THAT USE THIS GIANT SCOPE...
A.T.L.A.S
A.L.I.C.E
A.L.A.N*
*ACADEMICS LOVE ACRONYM NAMES
ONE OF THEM IS THE SEARCH FOR THE INFAMOUS HIGGS BOSON.
??
DIEGO, A 3rd YEAR THEORETICAL PHYSICS PH.D., EXPLAINS:
THERE'S A SET OF EQUATIONS CALLED THE STANDARD MODEL...
...THAT PRETTY MUCH DESCRIBES HOW MATTER INTERACTS WITH ITSELF (EXCEPT FOR GRAVITY)
$\mathcal{L}_g = -\frac{1}{4}(W^a_{\mu\nu}W^{a,\mu\nu} + B_{\mu\nu}B^{\mu\nu})$
$Z_\mu = \cos\theta_W W^3_\mu - \sin\theta_W B_\mu,$
$\mathcal{L}_{NC} = eJ^{em}_\mu A^\mu + \frac{g}{\cos\theta_W}(J^3_\mu - \sin^2\theta_W J^{em}_\mu)Z^\mu$
$\mathcal{L}_{QCD} = \overline{U}(\partial_\mu - ig_s G^a_\mu T^a)\gamma^\mu U + \overline{D}(\partial_\mu - ig_s G^a_\mu T^a)\gamma^\mu D.$
$\mathcal{L}_H = [(\partial_\mu - igW^a_\mu t^a - ig' Y_\phi B_\mu)\phi]^2 + \mu^2\phi^\dagger\phi - \lambda(\phi^\dagger\phi)^2,$
THE HIGGS BOSON IS THE ONLY FUNDAMENTAL PARTICLE PREDICTED BY THE MODEL THAT HASN'T BEEN OBSERVED.
g
g
t
H°
t̄
THE HIGGS IS SIGNIFICANT BECAUSE IT EXPLAINS WHY STUFF HAS MASS.
FOR ME IT'S THE RAMEN DIET.
WAIT, WE DON'T KNOW WHY STUFF HAS MASS??
WHAT IS MASS?
YOU JUST BLEW MY MIND.
I KNOW.
JORGE CHAM © 2008

WORKING ON SUCH A HIGH-PROFILE PROJECT MUST BE REALLY EXCITING, HUH?
COLLISIONS
PART 4
PHD TALES FROM THE ROAD
MEH. THERE ARE 2000 PEOPLE IN MY GROUP.
THAT'S NOT A RESEARCH TEAM ANYMORE, THAT'S A SMALL TOWN!
THE EXCITEMENT GETS A LITTLE DILUTED.
A SMALL TOWN COMPLETE WITH ITS OWN GOSSIP, DRAMA AND POLITICS...
TERESA'S ROLE IN THIS ARMY OF SCIENTISTS IS TO STAND IN THE FRONT LINES AGAINST THE ONSLAUGHT OF DATA THAT IS GENERATED.
SURROUNDING THE COLLISION POINT IS A GIGANTIC STRUCTURE CALLED A.T.L.A.S...
...MADE OF LAYERS UPON LAYERS OF SENSORS...
WITH OVER 160 MILLION CHANNELS OF DATA...
OUTPUTTING ABOUT 1 MILLION GIGABYTES PER SECOND.

TERESA WORKS ON ONE OF THE FIRST LAYERS OF FILTERS THAT SCREEN THE DATA IN REAL TIME FOR EVENTS THAT MATCH THE THEORETICAL PREDICTIONS.
WHAT HAPPENS TO ALL THE OTHER DATA?
WE THROW IT OUT.
BEING A GOOD PHYSICIST IS KNOWING HOW TO APPROXIMATE--
YOU HAVE TO DECIDE WHAT IS IMPORTANT AND WHAT CAN BE IGNORED.
APPARENTLY, THIS IS ALSO TRUE IN THEORY:
WE THROW OUT EQUATION TERMS ALL THE TIME. IN QUANTUM PHYSICS EVERY-THING IS POSSIBLE, BUT NOT EVERYTHING IS LIKELY.
REALIZING THIS OFTEN COMES AS A DISAPPOINTMENT TO MANY PEOPLE.
SOMETIMES, OUR EXPECTATIONS OF RESEARCH AND THE REALITIES OF IT COLLIDE.
YOU GROW UP THINKING SCIENCE IS THIS PURE THING,...
YAY SCIENCE!
...BUT WHEN YOU GET INTO IT YOU FIND OUT IT'S MESSY AND FULL OF GUESSES AND APPROXIMATIONS.
$%#* SCIENCE!
WE ALL THINK OUR RESEARCH IS BULLSH*T.
IF YOUR RESEARCH IS BULLSH*T, WHAT IS MINE??
JORGE CHAM © 2008

COLLISIONS
PART 5
PHD TALES FROM THE ROAD
WHAT IF..?
...YOU RUN THIS BIG EXPERIMENT AND YOU DON'T FIND ANYTHING?
HIGGS NOT FOUND.
THEN WE HAVE A LITTLE CHAT WITH THE THEORISTS...
GULP.
BUT EVEN FINDING NOTHING WOULD BE SIGNIFICANT.
PHYSICS IS ABOUT SHINING A LIGHT INTO THE UNKNOWN...
...AND WHILE THAT LIGHT CAN SHOW YOU THINGS YOU'D NEVER SEEN BEFORE...
YOU GOT ME.
HIGGS BOSON
NOT FINDING ANYTHING ALSO TELLS YOU SOMETHING ABOUT THE WORLD.
JORGE CHAM © 2008

OF COURSE, EVERY INSTRUMENT HAS ITS LIMITATIONS...
...WHICH MEANS YOU CAN'T REALLY BE SURE UNLESS YOU HAVE A POWERFUL ENOUGH TOOL.
EXCUSE ME
OUR JOB AS EXPERIMENTALISTS IS TO PUSH THE BOUNDARIES OF CONDITIONS UNDER WHICH YOU CAN SAY WITH CONFIDENCE WHAT IS...
...AND ISN'T THERE.
WHAT IF..?
...YOU RUN THIS BIG EXPERIMENT AND THE WORLD BLOWS UP?
HAHA, DON'T WORRY...
IT'S VERY UNLIKELY.
THESE KINDS OF COLLISIONS HAPPEN ALL THE TIME IN NATURE: IN THE SUN, THE ATMOSPHERE...
...AND WE'RE STILL HERE.
THIS IS JUST THE FIRST TIME IT'S MAN-MADE.
IT'S PROBABLY NOT THE END OF THE WORLD.
REALLY? I WAS HOPING TO END THIS COMIC WITH A BANG.

PHD TALES FROM THE ROAD PRESENTS:
"Jim"
JORGE CHAM © 2008
MY HOST A FEW MONTHS AGO FOR MY TALK AT EPFL (IN SWITZERLAND) WAS JIM, AN AMERICAN GETTING HIS PH.D. IN COMPUTER SCIENCE.
BON JOUR!
WHAT'S UP.
JIM DESCRIBES THE CIRCULAR LOGIC OF SWISS IMMIGRATION BUREAUCRACY:
"TO GET AN APARTMENT, YOU FIRST NEED A BANK ACCOUNT."
"...BUT TO GET A BANK ACCOUNT, YOU NEED A RESIDENCY CARD."
"BUT TO GET A RESIDENCY CARD, YOU NEED AN ADDRESS, WHICH YOU ONLY GET IF YOU HAVE AN APARTMENT!!"
I ASK JIM WHAT HE PLANS TO DO AFTER HE GRADUATES:
I'M GOING TO PACK MY BAGS AND VOLUNTEER FOR THE OBAMA CAMPAIGN!
WE ALL HAVE OUR MOTIVATIONS TO GRADUATE. HIS WAS A TIGHT DEADLINE: THE PRIMARIES WERE ALREADY UNDER WAY AT THE TIME.
CAN YOU FINISH IN TIME?
YES, I CAN.
JIM EXPLAINS THAT STAYING IN ACADEMIA DOESN'T REALLY INSPIRE HIM ANYMORE.
YOU HAVE TO BE A SALESMAN TO SURVIVE. IT'S ALL POLITICS.
FUND ME!!
$$!
BEING AN OBAMA SUPPORTER MYSELF, I WISH HIM LUCK:
WHAT ARE YOU GOING TO DO AFTER THE ELECTION?
UH...
HOPE

JORGE CHAM © 2008
PHD TALES FROM THE ROAD PRESENTS:
"2nd Desserts"
WHERE WERE YOU THE NIGHT OF THE FAMOUS ELECTION??
REPORTS ARE COMING IN FROM GRAD STUDENTS ALL OVER THE WORLD:
"UH, I WAS IN THE LAB"
"I WAS STUDYING FOR PRELIMS"
ME, I WAS AT A HOTEL IN ZURICH, JETLAGGED AND WATCHING IT ON TV.
VIRTUALLY EVERY CHANNEL WAS COVERING IT.
obama a la maison blanche!
...al fin, un presidente negro!
ich habe einen Traum...
THE WHOLE WORLD WAS WATCHING!
AT THE TRAIN STATION AT 5am, IT'S CLEAR I WASN'T THE ONLY ONE WHO HEARD THE NEWS.
OBAMA
AN AMERICAN WOMAN TRAVELING HOME LOOKED ECSTATIC.
I'M NOT EMBARRASSED TO SAY I'M FROM OHIO ANYMORE!
pant
pant
THAT AFTERNOON I GO TO OXFORD, WHERE THE AT-CAPACITY AUDITORIUM MAKES IT CLEAR WHO THE BIGGER CELEBRITY IS:
PLEASE WELCOME JORGE CHAM.
clap. clap.
clap.
OBAMA WON
WHOOO!!
YEAH!!!
WOO HOO!!
AFTER THE LECTURE, I WAS INVITED FOR DINNER AT HIGH TABLE IN TRINITY COLLEGE
DOES THE FOOD POP UP MAGICALLY FROM THE TABLE?
THAT'S CHRIST CHURCH.
I ASK MY HOST WHY EUROPE IS SO ENTHRALLED BY THIS ELECTION
THE U.S. IS LIKE OUR YOUNGER SIBLING.
THEY'RE MORE EXCITING, YET WE LOVE TO ROLL OUR EYES AT THEM.
BESIDES, SHE SAID, IT'S BEEN A FASCINATING STORY IN ITSELF, WITH INCREDIBLE CHARACTERS AND PERSONALITIES.

AFTER A 2-HOUR 5-COURSE MEAL, WE MOVE TO ANOTHER ROOM FOR "2nd DESSERT"
DON'T YOU PEOPLE EVER WORK?
THIS IS WORK.
I STRIKE A CONVERSATION WITH THE PERSON NEXT TO ME, A SENIOR GOVERNMENT DIPLOMAT, WHO OFFERS A MEASURED ASSESSMENT OF THE DAY'S EVENTS.
"HIS EXCELLENCY"?
WE CANNOT UNDERESTIMATE THE SIGNIFI-CANCE OF THIS ELECTION...
...BUT WE MUSTN'T OVERESTIMATE IT EITHER.
A PRESIDENT CAN ONLY DO SO MUCH.
THE U.S., HE SAYS, IS THE ONLY COUNTRY IN THE WORLD WHERE MAJOR CANDIDATES FOR OFFICE ARE CHOSEN BY THE PEOPLE (IN PRIMARIES), AND NOT BY BACK-ROOM POLITICAL PARTY MACHINATIONS.
THIS MUCH DEMOCRACY GIVES THE RESULTS LEGITIMACY, BUT NOT ALWAYS QUALITY.
AFTER ALL, THEY DID ELECT BUSH TWICE.
LATER THAT NIGHT, I GET AN E-MAIL FROM JIM, WHO DIDN'T FINISH HIS PH.D. BUT WENT TO VOLUNTEER ANYWAY:
WHAT A DAY! FIRST OBAMA WINS, AND NOW I'M IN A PHD COMIC!
I GUESS YOU DON'T NEED A PH.D. TO CHANGE THE WORLD.

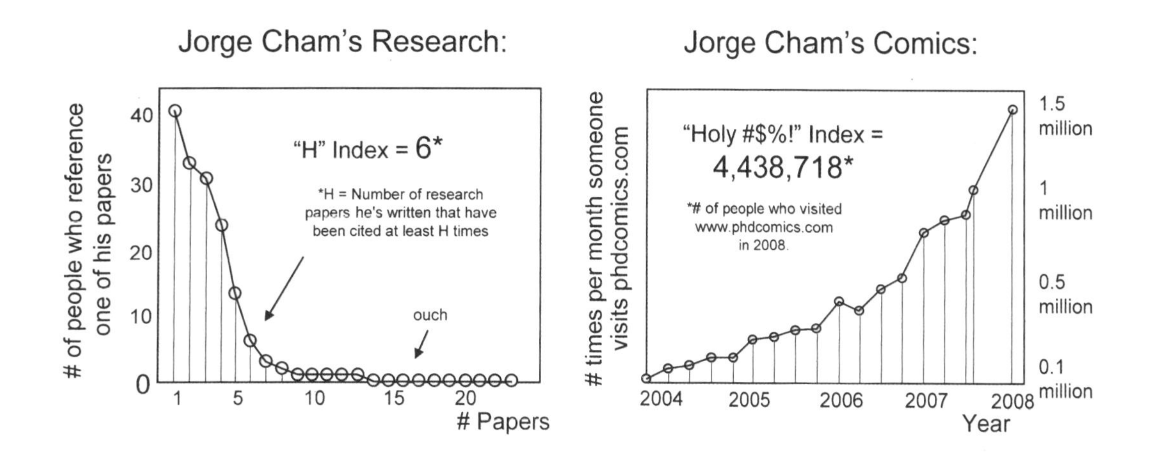

About the Author

Jorge Cham was born and raised in Panama. He got his B.S. from Georgia Tech and his M.S. and PhD from Stanford University, specializing in Robotics. He subsequently worked as an Instructor and Research Associate at Caltech for two years. *Piled Higher and Deeper* began in the Stanford Daily in 1997, and currently appears in over 30 newspapers and online, where it receives over 9 million page-views each month.

More info at *www.phdcomics.com*

Acknowledgements

Many thanks to the readers of PHD for supporting the comic and for providing many of the ideas for jokes in this book. PHD wouldn't exist without you! Oh, thanks also to my family and my beautiful life partner, Suelika.

Seminar BINGO!

To play, simply print out this bingo sheet and attend a departmental seminar.

Mark over each square that occurs throughout the course of the lecture.

The first one to form a straight line (or all four corners) must yell out to win!

SEMINAR BINGO

B	I	N	G	O
Speaker bashes previous work	Repeated use of "um…"	Speaker sucks up to host professor	Host Professor falls asleep	Speaker wastes 5 minutes explaining outline
Laptop malfunction	Work ties in to Cancer/HIV or War on Terror	"…et al."	You're the only one in your lab that bothered to show up	Blatant typo
Entire slide filled with equations	"The data *clearly* shows…"	FREE Speaker runs out of time	Use of Powerpoint template with blue background	References Advisor (past or present)
There's a Grad Student wearing same clothes as yesterday	Bitter Post-doc asks question	"That's an interesting question"	"Beyond the scope of this work"	Master's student bobs head fighting sleep
Speaker forgets to thank collaborators	Cell phone goes off	You've no idea what's going on	"Future work will…"	Results conveniently show improvement